SEEING
ANGELS

SEEING ANGELS

EMMA HEATHCOTE-JAMES

JB

JOHN BLAKE

Published by John Blake Publishing Ltd,
3 Bramber Court, 2 Bramber Road,
London W14 9PB, England

First published in paperback 2002

ISBN 1 904034 15 2

British Library Cataloguing-in-Publication Data:

A catalogue record for this book is
available from the British Library.

Typeset by t2

Printed and bound in Great Britain by
BookMarque Ltd, Croydon, Surrey.

3 5 7 9 10 8 6 4

Papers used by John Blake Publishing Limited are natural,
recyclable products made from wood grown in sustainable forests.
The manufacturing processes conform to the environmental
regulations of the country of origin.

I would like to dedicate this book to my grandmother, Eileen Dorothy Giles, who sadly could never see the finished version.

CONTENTS

ANGELS

God's motorcycle couriers. No request from the Almighty turned down. Not human quite - not divine quite. Can get quite a few on a pinhead. Usually invisible, often turn up just when you need one - but you don't usually realise they were there until they aren't. (NB Some churches don't believe in them, others never think about them, some meet them for breakfast every Tuesday)

Taken from *The Church-English Dictionary*

'The Alpha to Omega of Church Speak'

INTRODUCTION

WHY ANGELS? WHY NOW?

*'Britain is experiencing Angel Fever,
with thousands… claiming to have seen, smelled or
touched an angel. You can even take lessons on how
to summon one yourself'*[1]

IN THE PAST, angelic visions and visitations have occurred, it seemed, to an elite few. Those few tended to be the more eccentric, artistic and creative members of society, such as William Blake, John Milton, Emanuel Swedenborg and Joseph Smith, the founder of Mormonism. However, over the past decade there has been a surge in angelic profile – both in terms of the commercialism of angels and of their alleged visitations. This renaissance, which probably stemmed from a sentimental, late Victorian revival, began in the early 1990s in the USA and has since flooded over to Britain. Angels have invaded the media, through fashion, films, TV talk shows, music, advertising, magazines, newspapers (including Page Three) and, of course, the internet. Since this time, it appears that increasing numbers of British people are claiming to have had angel encounters, leading to what many social observers are terming the 'angel phenomenon'.

According to a survey in *Time Magazine*, 69% of American people believe in angels and a staggering 46% feel they have a guardian angel.[2] Moreover, the greatest growth area of belief is in angels, with one in three people attesting that they have actually witnessed the presence of such a celestial being. Such figures astounded me, and became the spark that ignited this research. However, I wanted to expand on this, to delve into the issue even more deeply and ask the question: are British attitudes the same? Were people in the UK having similar experiences – and if so, would they be prepared to share them with me? This, for the past four years, has been the framework of my doctorate; this book is a culmination of its data and findings.

As yet there is no UK poll on angels comparable to the

American one. The closest comparison is a survey by David Hay[3], until recently the Director of the Alister Hardy Research Centre at Manchester University, on religious experience in which the results for the US and England are much the same (one-third of each population believed they had had a powerful religious experience). Working along these lines, I would imagine that statistics of angel encounters would be near parallel as well.

Angels: the in-thing!

Today, stories of angel appearances are commonplace; the internet features hundreds of sites devoted to angels, with thousands of people accessing these sites each day. Variations on the angelic theme are distributed and circulated ad infinitum: 'At AngelHaven.com you can feel the presence of Angels. Come inside and share your angelic experiences, visit our angel chat rooms, send an Angel Gram, ask questions about angels, read weekly columns from inspired authors, shop for angels...'[4] Many people now wear guardian angel pins; there are numerous angel books and angel newsletters, and there is at least one monthly angel magazine. There are angel collectibles – dolls, teddy bears, plates, paintings and figurines – not to mention the vast array of stationery on offer. Shops and mail-order catalogues have appeared in the UK dedicated exclusively to stocking angel memorabilia.[5] In addition to this, television programmes are increasingly including accounts of angelic encounters (Carol Vorderman's Mysteries series, Kilroy, GMTV, The Big Breakfast all provide examples), while sales of paranormal magazines and literature are healthy. One can find angel specialists who can divulge information about their client's personal guardian angel either via letter, telephone, the internet or in person. From these specialists, people learn the name of their guardian angel and (for an even larger fee), may obtain a sketch of what their angel looks like. Even in the UK there are angel group therapy sessions in which one can communicate with angels for help with problems as well as meditation workshops to enable visualisation of personal guardians.[6]

In a word, angels are the in-thing at the moment. Unlike most in-things that spread over here from the States, however, they have not been a five-minute wonder. Near-death experiences and alien abductions (to name but two well-known types of otherworldly encounters) all had their peak in Britain, but, although both types of experience are still being recorded, as far as the media are concerned they turned out to be simply fads that did not last. Because of this, I chose the topic of angels thinking the wave must surely be on the verge of crashing, or that it certainly would as soon as we hit the new millennium. But I was wrong. Angels are still 'in'; indeed, they may well be even more 'in' than they were back then!

The whole concept of religion has had me spellbound since the seed of fascination was sewn in my schooldays. Religion is something that affects every one of us, be it as a believer, non-believer, nominal follower or agnostic. I was particularly interested in primitive religion during my undergraduate days, intrigued by questions such as: where did religion start? What were the first philosophies? And where did the ideas of a god, or gods, evolve? It was during my first degree in Theology, at Birmingham University that I became aware of the fascination with angels that was starting to sweep the UK. From writing a short dissertation on the subject back in 1997, it became clear to me that there was more to the phenomenon than I had first supposed, and I stayed on to expand the work into an anthropological Masters degree, which in turn led to the PhD I am currently writing up.

Unfortunately, the stigma of reading for a Theology degree

is still rife – people often assume that I am a stuffy-sandals-and-brown-rice brigade member, or a narrow-minded religious bigot; far from it (and I have yet to find someone in my area who is!). For my academic work, I tend to sit on the fence and write as an agnostic. I believe that others believe in angelic experiences, but I really do not know whether I do or not. From what I have ascertained, the evidence is inconclusive. Psychology provides many theories to account for visions or other kinds of otherworldly encounters, but on the other side of the coin, psychological and medical theories have not provided answers that could explain away every experience I have investigated. And this is an important point to remember. Most of us today tend to put our faith in the 'physical' world, believing there to be some form of scientific explanation for everything. On the other hand, many of us are not ashamed to admit that sometimes there are seemingly no rational or logical explanations for things. Indeed, over the past few years I have researched and witnessed weeping icons, simulacra of Christ and the Blessed Virgin Mary, stigmata, psychic healing and various types of religious experiences and visions. I have also looked at and researched new religious movements. As very much a people person, I think the bottom line of my interests is the way in which religion affects us – as a society and as individuals. In the case of this study, the effect a religious experience has on its recipients and the life-changes, or the new ways of thought, that stem from it.

A brief summary of this project

My angel research started out as a humble paragraph in local church newsletters – it seemed the most logical place to begin. The local press and various religious publications took an interest, which soon caught the imagination of the tabloids, broadsheets and national glossies. I was invited on to various radio shows, particularly around Christmas time, to talk about the research and what exactly was going on here, and soon there were angel articles all over the media and adverts asking for people to write to me with their experiences.

Finding a place to begin was the hardest thing about the project. Angel literature is in abundance today – copious amounts have been written on angelology and angels in art – but academically, aside from work on mystical and religious experiences, there was a void of information concerning angelic visions and experience. This was not a calculated topic choice; it was a combination of luck, coincidence and good humour. After noting the American survey mentioned earlier, I suggested to my university, in quite a tongue-in-cheek manner, the idea of researching the topic of angelic experiences, eager to see the reaction. 'If anyone can pull it off, you can', came the reply. A red rag to a bull I'm afraid... and there began the project.

Always one for a challenge, and one to rarely admit defeat, I decided the aim was to assess the frequency and nature of angelic experiences throughout Britain. I set about collecting personal testimonies from those who believed they had encountered angelic beings or had had some angel-related experience. There were already a handful of books on the market outlining such stories, but the books either contained fewer than 60 or so accounts, or siphoned off experiences to report just those that were in line with biblical teaching. From this, it was apparent such data collection could be achieved on a small scale – and originally that was all I intended to do. The media interest surrounding this work enabled it to develop into what it is today.

It was therefore important that the adverts I placed would reach out equally to both believers and non-believers – I wanted to see whether such experiences were as prevalent in non-orthodox communities as they were in those of different religious communities. Being an impoverished student, I began the work in the form of taking out simple 'Have you seen an angel?' adverts in local Birmingham magazines and free newspapers:

> Have you seen an angel? Research student wishes to hear from anybody who has encountered an angelic presence. Please write, outlining your experience and providing details of your age and faith at the time of the experience and any after-effect/feeling you have had as a result, to...

My naivety showed and it soon became apparent by the handful of replies that this was not the way to proceed... One local newspaper charged advertisers if an address was to be used, but provided free ads if just a telephone contact was given. After ending several very difficult phone calls and quickly changing the number, it occurred to me that perhaps the wording was rather ambiguous, and unknowingly bore sexual connotations! The imagination of some Brummies was outrageous!

Fortunately, the now ridiculous advert had caught the eye of a couple of serious journalists. The local paper in which I had originally advertised wrote an article that aroused more interest locally. A news scout passed an article onto the broadsheets and the Church press also agreed to publish small paragraphs outlining the work I was doing. Soon, this escalated into articles being printed throughout the national media and, eventually, an edition of the BBC's Everyman[7] series being dedicated to the subject of encounters with angels. As part of the pre-publicity for the latter, I also spoke on television and radio internationally. The topic particularly caught the imagination of people in New Zealand and Australia; however, the experiences received from other countries have not been included in this research which, for now, is strictly limited to residents of the UK. I did avoid the afternoon TV talk shows though, out of choice. The topic breeds interest and I wanted to protect all the people who had written to me. After all, they had written in confidence, assuming that their experiences would be used as part of credible research, not to have their names broadcast from a TV screen, with the potential to be teased that might well result. Over the years there have been many calls from frustrated researchers, some literally begging, who pleaded that even if I didn't want to take part in a show, could I still provide them with ten or so people who had had angelic experiences. That fact alone proves how hard people who have had such encounters are to track down and how fortunate I am that so many wrote to me. When the programme came out, consent was sought from each individual involved, as it has been for this book. But even so, I do feel very protective of every person who participated. I know how easy this topic is to make fun of (heavens, there has been many a conference in which I have ended up fighting my corner!) and I wanted total control over it.

The first major article in the non-religious press to outline the work I was doing and what I was hoping to achieve featured in the local Birmingham Post[8]. During the interview for the piece, I was asked if I personally had seen an angel – in honesty, I replied that I did not know, but that we all experience striking coincidences in our lives and that it would be lovely to think that I had. Hesitantly, I proceeded to tell the interviewer about an experience I had had in Egypt.

The Summer of 1995 I spent travelling around Egypt and Israel, and it was mid-trip that I experienced what could perhaps be interpreted as an angelic presence. A night hike up Mount Sinai had been organised. The climb up was tiring but well worth it – the views of the sunrise were spectacular.

Without thinking twice, a friend and I wandered off to take photographs; inevitably, we lost track of time and when we returned to the spot where we had left the group it turned out they had begun the descent down without us, presuming we had gone on ahead.

The journey down was very disorientating, especially since the climb up had been in total darkness and partly on camel. It soon turned out that we were all alone, with no one in front of us, nor behind, and the prospect of having to climb the treacherous path down by ourselves filled us both with dread — the two excited explorers fast became a couple of terrified tourists! We had taken the wrong path, and huge boulders precariously placed created a dangerous way down. We began to pray, knowing little else to do — I have never done it before, but I hysterically cried out aloud. It was after this that several coincidental things happened. Firstly we kept seeing a person dressed in a long white garment on ledges below us. At the time, I believed it to be our group leader who, like most Arabs, was in fact wearing a white robe. But each time we reached the point where we had seen him, there was nothing there. This happened several times. Then, literally out of nowhere, a beautiful young couple appeared behind a big rock. It struck me immediately how manicured and well dressed they were despite the fact that they must have been climbing for six hours or so — the woman especially looked like she had stepped from the cover of *Vogue*, with sheered denim hotpants, and lustrous long brown hair! Strangely, she spoke perfect English. Their calm overawed us, making us stop and take in the view and appreciate the situation in which we found ourselves. Helping us over the worst terrain, they accompanied us to the bottom where we found our group and our *very* distraught leader who thought he'd lost us! We turned to thank the couple but they were nowhere to be seen.

It was not until we arrived back at the camp later that day that a Muslim suggested that what we had witnessed – the white figures and then the French couple – were angels.

Personally I have never regarded this as an angelic encounter – though it is the closest experience I have ever had to it.

The theological answer would be that through prayer we had asked for God's protection and were granted just that – guardianship and security in what was a potentially dangerous situation. Some believe that angels operate on a different frequency to ours, and have to 'tune in' in order for us to understand their presence. As the Muslim gentleman told us, we obviously did not fully recognise the figure in white, mistaking it to be someone we knew, so they transformed into the guise of the couple – what is true is that, although they looked as human as us, there were distinct points about them that made them seem different (such as their calm, beauty and sudden disappearance at the end).

Alternatively, and more prosaically, we had been climbing for over seven hours with little rest, we were hungry and dehydrated (the others had taken our packs down with them) and we had both hallucinated at the same time, seeing perhaps what we wanted to see. A combination of the heat, lack of food and water and intent desire to will an experience would no doubt have added to the occurrence. Perhaps this is simply what we witnessed. Psychologically, the Catholic image of a guardian angel appearing in times of trouble may have been impressed deep in my mind since I was a young child. At the time, on Mount Sinai I was obviously very distressed and my fertile mind may have seized upon such a suppressed image in a bid to restore calm and reduce panic. Who knows? There are many possible explanations, but this does not take the actual experience away.

Whatever the origin of the experience is, it has always remained with me. Unfortunately the climax of my story is not as great as many which I have received. I have not, like some respondents, had a calling to the ministry, nor have I become a different person. So whether or not this was a real encounter, a vision, hallucination or just a figment of our imaginations, I cannot and will not ever be able to tell.

Originally, I was reluctant to use my own beliefs as an angle for the article, especially with the research being from an academic viewpoint – an area with which my personal beliefs shouldn't interfere. However, the very first reply that I received, from a Judith Shrimpton, quickly dispelled all uncertainty:

> I would like to say... how courageous I feel you are to publish your experience. We are living in an age of scepticism and this type of experience... is inclined to be dismissed as eccentric fantasy and the propagator written off as 'unbalanced' or a 'bit of a nut'. I often feel this attitude inhibits people [from] talking and sharing their experiences and I can only hope that your article might have broken down a few taboos...'

After this came more replies, all saying the same thing, which made me believe that in this instance, it was the correct way to have approached things. Presumably, I came across as being on the same level as others who have encountered an angelic presence. However, the article certainly portrayed my beliefs and from that enabled others to feel the desire to retell their story, knowing that they would not be faced with scepticism or pessimism – 'Thank you for taking the subject seriously – but not solemnly! – and for giving us the chance to tell our stories.'

The media interest reiterates the aura of myth and fantasy that engulfs the subject of angels, even in the 20th century.

What seems to be perfectly normal in biblical contexts seems over the top and unreal in today's world. Most people today are sceptical and assume anyone believing in angels (let alone seeing them!) to be slightly bizarre or even eccentric... just as the article speculated. However, through the personal accounts that I had received, I think I have shown this not to be the case.

Why angels? Why now?

So, after spending the past four years studying 'people who claim to see angels', the first question that springs to most minds is simply 'Why Angels?' The vast resurgence of belief in angels and their appeal fascinates me, as do the people who claim to have had angelic experiences. But are experiences solely, 'for those who choke too easily on God and His rules; angels are the handy compromise, all fluff and meringue, kind, non-judgmental. And they are available to everyone like aspirin?' Or is there more to it? I would argue there is...

I assume I have experienced as many coincidental events – be they prompted by fate or luck – as anyone, but never have I put them down to angelic intervention, quite simply because nothing that's ever happened to me has come close to fitting the spine-tingling accounts included later in these pages. When people have an angel experience they just *know* it was an angel – there is no question about it.

USA–UK

Most trends spread to the UK after achieving huge popularity in America. Angels were no different, achieving their peak in the US during the early 1990s – as The Wall Street Journal reported some years back:

> There is resurgence among a diverse US population who believe that guardian angels not only exist, but

claim to have a working relationship with them. Angelology seminars and lectures, and a noticeable rise in publications about angelic contact, indicate a growing acceptance of angelic presence in everyday life. Accounts of angelic contact contain common elements that angels are incorporeal, sexless, highly intelligent, able to move at the speed of thought, full of warmth and joy, are co-operative not competitive...[9]

An entire book could easily be dedicated to answering the question 'What is an angel experience?', something that will be explored more thoroughly in the following chapter. Such a question is hard to address concisely, as angels are seen in many different forms – not just the simple apparition of a blond-haired male (or female) with wings in white robes that many people imagine. The diversity is vast – responses ranged from a scientist seeing an eight-foot angel with enormous wings, to a Jewish hospice worker who sees angels all the time – especially on public transport. One respondent recalls being saved from a potentially fatal swimming accident whilst another Muslim gentleman talks about seeing an angel that looked like Jesus, an experience that gave him strength and hope before his heart by-pass operation. A blind woman claims to 'see angels as [the sighted] see people'; a second lady talks about being 'wafted up a flight of steps and through a closed door' as a car sped out of control towards her, and to have felt feathers behind her knees during the experience. Another woman recalls being protected by a 'woman who disappeared' as she walked lost and afraid through the subways; the list goes on...

It seems that the most common contemporary image of angels stems from the late Victorian era – what I shall term a 'traditional angel', the type we put on top of our Christmas tree, or that appears on greeting cards. This is usually a being dressed in white or in shining apparel, with wings and a halo, stunningly beautiful in every feature. Perhaps not surprisingly, in my studies I have found that it is these traditional-style angels that feature most prominently in people's experiences.

However, an astonishing amount of people saw angels that appeared in human form. Experiences of this nature generally include a 'person' arriving unexpectedly and almost out of the blue in a time of desperate need or crisis. Always when the angels have finished their work they disappear instantly. Everyone who has had such an encounter states that there is something 'extra-special' about the person, but can not put his or her finger on exactly what it is.

Theologians maintain that although angels can and do appear in a human form, their image is not necessary for their presence to be there. Some people, for example, feel a presence that they attribute to being an angel, whereas others do not actually see or feel anything at all and are only aware of an angel being present when others point it out – a well-documented example of this would be that of Alice Z, a young Seventh-Day Adventist, who was selling literature door to door in a hostile neighbourhood in the Philippines. Alice was welcomed into one house, where the guard dogs seemed friendly rather than fierce. Two chairs were set out for her rather than one and the lady of the house addressed the second chair as if someone were there, remarking to Alice that her 'companion' certainly looked becoming in white. Alice herself was not aware that anyone else was there, but various individual witnesses all insisted that they saw a figure in white with her.

To some extent, the increased interest in angels might have ultimately reduced the impact of such stories, by de-sensitising people to them. However, I still believe that, despite broad media coverage, such accounts are no more or less potent than those experienced in previous years. New Age thinking has undoubtedly spawned much of the current interest in angels; however, I think there is a lot more to it than that alone. For example, I do not believe that angels are a recent phenomenon at all. In fact, this work shows that a large percentage of people who are writing to me now had their experiences as long as sixty years ago, although, it is only now that they feel able to discuss them. Others have written to me recounting stories of their parents' or grandparents' experiences that have been passed on down to them.

Others don't actually 'see' anything. One lady was waiting to cross a busy main road when a hand grabbed her shirt collar and prevented her from crossing – as she turned to see who had been so rude to grab hold of her, a car sped past – had she have gone into the road she believes she'd have been hit by it. But there was no one in sight who could possibly have touched her... encounters such as this are surprisingly common, as we shall see in chapter three.

So why the sudden surge of interest in angelology? There are surely many contributory factors, including pre-millennium fever, a phenomenon that is connected to an increased interest in New Age beliefs and spirituality. Some people attribute the growing fascination with all things angelic to the basic decline of mainstream religion, believing such enigmatic experiences are simply one manifestation of humanity's need for spiritual fulfilment. Put more simply, given the fact that such a large percentage of our generation has grown up with no religious faith, the angel phenomenon is perhaps simply the manifestation of man's need for 'something else greater than us' – a prime factor, or need, or yearning apparent in all religions from the year dot.

Personally, I believe the concept of globalisation to be the key reason. For example, the internet enables people to circulate their experiences, beliefs and stories to others all around the world – and the more something is spoken about, the more barriers and taboos are being broken down. I certainly do not believe angel sightings and experiences have become more common – they have always been around, it is just that the topic can be spoken about more openly nowadays.

Who has these experiences? The simple answer would be anyone – there are no commonalities whatsoever between respondents. I have received letters from doctors and nurses who had witnessed angels within a hospital ward, policemen, academics, clergy, bankers, a physicist, barristers and council workers to name but a few. The message is clear: people from all cultural backgrounds, faiths and professions are having angelic experiences. However, all felt the need to justify their claims with sentences such as:

> … I really am a sensible, matter-of-fact sort of person, not prone to hysteria or wild imagination!

> At the time, my eyesight was 'spot on' and I hadn't been 'taking anything'. I am not interested in healing crystals etc…

> I can not stress enough the fact that I certainly do not suffer from any sort of neurological, nervous or mental disorder…

One respondent was quite emphatic in his letter:

> I am writing as a direct result of yesterday's piece in the Daily Telegraph concerning your research, and should like to make some points clear at the start.

1) I do not take, have never taken and will never take drugs, other than administered and prescribed ones; indeed, I loathe the very subject, and have told my G.P. that, whatever sort of pain I might be in, [...] she is not to prescribe cannabis if the stuff receives a green light for medicinal purposes.

2) I am not considered mentally unstable; even I do not regard myself in that category, although ward staff whom I have known for years have tired of trying to get me to take things – or myself – seriously.

3) At the time of the incident, alcohol could not possibly have been involved.

There have long been rumours of angels being sighted from planes and spacecraft. It has even been reported that pilots have seen and indeed photographed angels in the sky; before one picture was taken, the crew had radioed the control tower to say they were having great difficulty in handling the plane – believing at least one engine was failing, they were preparing for an emergency landing. Moments later they said they saw an unidentified object that appeared to be flying beside the plane. Tapes of their conversation reveal that at one point the pilots were almost frantic with worry, but quickly became very calm – with perhaps even a sense of serenity in their voices. On the tower tape, the pilot describes an angel hovering just outside the front window of the plane. One of the crew said he was going to take a photograph with a camera of the pilots in the cockpit – he took several exposures but the angel was only visible in one of them.[10]

According to inside sources at the space centres in Houston, Texas and Cape Canaveral, Florida, angels have been sighted by astronauts during most space missions and one astronaut even claims angels followed him back to Earth.[11]

27

NASA astronauts hit the headlines in *The Sun* (not to be confused with the UK tabloid of the same name), under the headline 'NASA Crew sees Angels in Space'. Over the years, NASA astronauts say they have encountered hundreds of the heavenly beings while in orbit – one astronaut even claims one hovered over him on a space walk.

If angelic encounters have been reported from such a variety of cultures, the implications are vast. So many theories and boundaries could be broken down. Theoretically, it can be argued that experiences that include a traditional-style angel are culturally determined – the person is seeing what they have been culturally conditioned to expect. A Muslim, for example, who is not familiar with the portrayal of angels in art familiar to Christians, should, logically speaking, not see a traditional-style angel, but rather one that drew upon Islamic imagery. However, the experience of Anver Hajee, which we will hear about in chapter eight, does not accord with this theory.

With the surge of interest in belief in angels and personal encounters, many new books on angel-related subjects have entered the market. It was brought to my attention well before I began that problems might arise due to the differences found in the older, biblical and theological writings and of those more recent publications connected with New Age thinking and spirituality. Another problem connected with books containing personal accounts of experience is that the information tends to be biased. Because the research material had been collected and collated by the book's author and not myself, I did not know the statistics and number of experiences that such stories have been taken from; neither did I have access to the stories that had been excluded, or know why they had been so. Therefore, I planned early on not to use such sections from that area of literature in my work, and to work from my own material instead. All experiences used in this database are ones that have been sent to me. The only exclusions are a handful of time-wasters and ones in which I believe the person to have been taking medication or drugs.

With my research and this book, I have sought to produce something that will complement and add to the literature around at the moment on angels and angelic visions. The market so far seems to consist either of material written by Christians or produced by Church publishing houses, or to be narrative accounts. Coming from an academic background, I felt I wanted to add something that would delve slightly deeper into the area, but also be accessible for everyone. Hopefully this work will fill the gap and benefit those who have had an angelic experience and those who are interested in the phenomenon as well as those who are carrying out similar work in the field.

However, before we begin, one problem we have to address is a simple 'What is an angel?' If one were to create a straw poll, no two people would give the same answer. After discussing this ambiguity and its problems over a conference dinner, I asked the other assembled delegates how they envisaged an angel's appearance – a great topic to cause debate! It proved that the idea of angels is deeply intertwined with spirits, ghosts, energies and other more recent New Age ideas about light. The following chapter will explore all of the different experiences that people have defined as being angelic in source.

The following experiences and statistics are taken from the first 350 accounts sent to me. They do not necessarily reflect my own views; they are merely a reproduction of the data I have been working with. These are the results so far...

ANGELS: THE GREAT CHAMELEONS

'… a shining figure about eight foot tall. It seemed to be made of beaten gold but I soon realised it was just solid light'

A S BRIEFLY ALLUDED to in the introduction, it seems that
angels may appear to people in varying guises. At one
end of the angelic spectrum, some have reported being
'embraced' by an invisible pair of wings, or being 'surrounded by
a smile'. At the other, angels have been described as 'warrior-like
with a vast stature and broad chest and limbs... he was dressed
in armour – like that of a Roman centurion – and his strength I
imagine would have made Samson appear childlike.'

In between the two spectrums are myriad other forms and
feelings associated with an angelic presence, such as the sound
of choirs, voices proclaiming messages and forces physically
moving people out of danger. Many people believe that angels
have appeared to them simply as a sensation or feeling (be it
internal or external) or by sending a white feather.

Angelic shape, size and colour could indeed reflect the
respondent's cultural background. Just as Jesus is seen as brown
in Ethiopian visions and white in Caucasian ones, we might
expect white, middle-class, church-going Britons to see Aryan
beings. Only three of the people who responded to this study
saw an angel in a non-traditional form. One described 'a white
Indian with a turban' when she was giving birth in England.
Other experiences of non-traditional angels tended to happen
abroad while travelling. In these visions, an angel in human
form took on the guise of a native of that country.

The following chart has been collated from the 350 letters
received for this research project and shows the various
categories of what people have attributed to being an angel
experience. Indeed, there are many more categories, but for a
straightforward presentation I have simplified it to the above.
In some cases, more than one category was involved in the

experience – for example when the vision of an angel was accompanied by a beautiful fragrance. For the sake of presentation, though, the results have been simplified. If, for example, a traditional angel or figure in human form was seen and a voice heard, the visionary experience was regarded as outweighing the audible or other sensory experiences.

How People See Angels

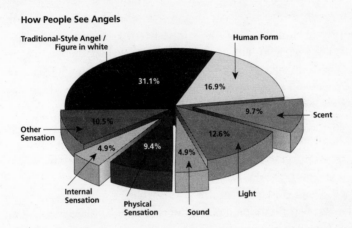

Just over 31% of respondents to this study reported seeing a *traditional-style angel*. In this category I combined all those who described seeing a beautiful ethereal being resembling something taken from Renaissance or Pre-Raphaelite art – a figure dressed in robes, usually white and glistening. A typical description of such a being would be along the following lines:

> She glows, she looks rather like a Pre-Raphaelite goddess in a Burn-Jones painting... She wears a light, long robe and a jewelled collar, she has an aquiline nose; [...] I could not say what colour her hair and eyes are, but they are perfect. All this really makes me sound like I am quite mad, but I really am not.

Occasionally the description varied a little:

> The dress was not white but of heavy blue or greenish
> brocade buttoned at the neck and there was just the
> suggestion of wing tips.

The vision sometimes seemed to be radiating light, a feature
that was sometimes depicted as being a halo. I also added in
those who saw a figure in white, whether they saw wings or
not. Some who wrote, after stating they had seen an angel,
may have failed to mention wings as they had thought that this
point would be obvious, though those who described the wings
did so with magnificent imagery:

> ... and I was surprised that they really did have wings,
> even more so that these wings reached from above
> their heads to the ground.

> ... sitting on the rail behind us were two girl angels –
> one with long wavy hair, one with shorter hair. Their
> wings were spread protectively over us.

> ... very suddenly an angel appeared. The figure itself
> did not seem to have importance – I do not remember
> a face – just two absolutely massive wings – quite
> extraordinary. As I was seeing this I was relating it to
> my husband. I remarked how large, how beautiful
> these wings were. It seemed the wings were of the
> greatest importance. Very suddenly (just as the 'angel'
> had come) it disappeared.

Although all of the angels mentioned in the Scriptures are male,
images of angels in art almost always depict females. This is

likely to be an attempt to convey the beauty inherent in the concept of the angelic being. It is also true that while referred to as male, angels are traditionally regarded as asexual and therefore are often seen as having an effeminate radiance, setting this divine beauty apart from mortal beauty. In line with this, it might be expected that the majority of people who had had an angelic experience would report that the otherworldly figure was female. In fact, most angels appeared as androgynous, though some have reported otherwise:

> I refer to my angel as male as my memory was of an adult with a flat chest rather than having a female bosom. I could see straight through him, as I could see the chest of drawers behind him. I think he had wings (or I wouldn't have been certain he was an angel). I think his hair came to just below his ears and he wore a single, loose garment. I couldn't see how long this was, as I was lying down. I couldn't see his feet.

Angels don't seem to be any particular dimension, though often they are described as being of a considerable size: 'his presence seemed to fill the room to the extent that nothing else could possibly get through the door unless the angel decreed'; others were 'enormous, at least seven feet tall'.

Only a handful of letters talked of seeing cherubim or other types of angels. June Calvert's experience occurred when she was a young girl of about 12 and she was quite ill with the mumps: 'I woke one night not feeling too well, I remember wanting to go to sleep but finding it very hard to sleep again, when two sweet angel faces, that's all, with little wings, seemed to comfort me back to sleep. I always remember this when anyone speaks of angels'.

Dawn Downey's experience occurred in September 1997:

We were living in our last home, a modern house... I went downstairs to eat my breakfast and watch the television news. The house was mainly open-plan and the dining area had a large picture window that faced east. The morning sun would stream through this window and light the large living room. On this morning I was sat on the sofa watching TV-AM and while I was eating my breakfast I looked away from the television to the part of the carpet illuminated by the morning sun. I know that there could be many reasonable explanations to describe what I saw, I even thought that somehow the sun had reflected an image from the television to the carpet but I really know that I had an angel sitting about five feet away from me on my living-room floor. This was a child of about eighteen months. He was wearing a cotton smock, I could see the gathers around the neck and on the sleeves. He had corn blonde hair with curls at the back of his head; as a mother of a small child I knew he had never had his hair cut because these were 'baby curls'. He had that wonderful skin that only small children possess and I could see the creases at the bends of his knees and wrists. We looked at each other for what seemed like hours, but was obviously [only] a few seconds. He was faintly illuminated, which I thought was due to the sunlight, but [he] seemed more golden. I can remember smiling at him and he just disappeared. I went upstairs to [my husband] Colin, woke him up and told him but he just laughed it off, as have several other people. I felt a great sense of warmth when this child, who looked like a cherub, was in my house.

Seeing an angel in *human form* is by no means a new concept and this is reflected in the fact that 17% of respondents saw a vision of this nature. Some of these contemporary angel-humans give messages, whilst others act as inconspicuous superheroes who use this non-threatening form of disguise to rescue individuals from a precarious situation, before dissolving back into nothingness. They never quite disappear in a puff of smoke, nor do they need a telephone box to get changed, but when the individual turns to thank them they are never there. An angel in human form is different to the more traditional figure in white. This is an entity dressed as a person, most usually in modern-day clothes. It appears, performs a deed and then disappears. However, the angel-human usually has something distinct about it – be it piercing blue eyes, a dramatic feature, immense beauty or a superhuman quality such as immense strength. It often imparts a message that turns out to have been a prophecy, as happened to Win Bairstow:

> I am an eighty-three-year-old [science] graduate, very down to earth and not given to flights of imagination. I had an otherwise inexplicable encounter in West Africa for which I can find no other explanation than [that] the man who warned me of danger was an angel. In 1964 I was teaching science and mathematics in a remote part of the Eastern Province of Sierra Leone, Kailahun, near the borders with Liberia and Guinea. It was necessary for official purposes that I should travel to Freetown, the capital. Not only was this a long, hazardous journey, but there are twenty-three different languages used in the country, so I took with me two of my students, both aged about eighteen, who between them knew all the languages in the villages and towns en route and could help with minor mechanical problems.

Before setting out at daybreak we sat in my Volkswagen and prayed for protection etc. In the heat of the day, when many Africans sleep, we were travelling down a straight, empty road with no villages for miles when a tall African, dressed in long, flowing white robes and white head gear flagged us down. The two youths in the back seat, urgently said, 'Don't stop Mrs Bairstow', but I did.

Astonishingly, this man was alone, not near any side road and obviously from his immaculate robes was not a hunter or worker. Even more astonishing was the fact that he spoke in perfect English, with a rich voice. The only other Africans I met with such good pronunciations had a Mercedes Benz – he hadn't even a bike!

He said to me, 'Madam, when you come to the end of this road you will turn right to cross the river: the bridge has been damaged but it is not obvious. Get out of your car and inspect [it], then you will know how you can cross safely.'

I thanked him and drove on a considerable distance. The youths behind me talked excitedly in the Mendi language but I sat there baffled!
Of course, he was right! The students crossed by foot – in case!

Ten per cent of respondents reported smelling a *scent* – 'a perfume, so beautiful – a real bouquet of flowers'; 'I always get a certain smell (of potpourri) before she appears and all the messages have been meaningful and accurate'. This type of experience is especially common around death, especially occurring to relatives of the dying near to the moment of death – this subject will be examined in more detail in chapter seven, 'Heaven Scent'.

Medical theories have been put forward suggesting this smell is a natural and common occurrence. Such arguments do not tally, however, with some of the stories that describe a sweet floral smell – a perfume like nothing the person has ever smelt before or since, especially to a relative who is *not* in the presence of the dying at the time, but perhaps back at home or halfway around the world:

> On the day my mother died in 1952 I smelt an intense smell of fresh flowers – all separate and identifiable. No one else in the family could smell them.

> Some years ago a very dear friend died. On returning home one day and entering the bedroom, there was a very strong perfume of flowers. My husband was convinced I had spilt some of my perfume. It was not so. A few weeks after my husband passed away, I entered the hall of my flat; the smell of perfume was terrific. It really is quite a mystery

Light is a contributory factor in all mystical experiences, so it is not surprising that so many people reported it when describing angelic experiences. Psychological theories would discount such experiences, stating that such light is caused by hyperactive firing in the brain's visual cortex. Whatever the cause, 13% of people in my study reported seeing a light, or perhaps a beam of light, which they attributed to being an angelic force or presence. As Vicky Copestake, an angel artist, told me, 'the angels that I paint are not the angels that I see, but the angels that I feel. The ones I see are small, luminous, very bright, they flitter – that's a good word – they flitter.' Some have reported being temporarily 'engulfed' in light, such as Elsie Dent. Elsie's experience happened back in 1944 when she was 24. Her husband had been on the continent since D-Day, so she was very sensitive to the fact he was in constant danger. Then, one night in bed, she was aware that she was surrounded by great light and recalls thinking 'my eyes are shut – how can I be seeing this?'

> ... suddenly a voice said 'Jack Yeoman' – not my husband's name, but my cousin's (a navigator in the RAF). There was a period of confusion, more lights, and then nothing. I opened my eyes and it was dark and surprisingly I was not afraid – it all seemed normal as if I had had a glimpse at... another world. Next morning my mother had a call from my aunt to say Jack had not returned from a flight over town called Hamm in Germany... said he was only 'missing' and there was still hope. After the call... I replied to my mother 'No, he died last night'... He never was found.

A similar experience ran thus: '... then an incredible bright light came into the bedroom... it was the sort of brightness that you could sense through closed eyelids (I didn't open my eyes).' One woman described seeing a '... a shining figure about eight foot tall. It seemed to be made of beaten gold but I soon realised it was just solid light.'

Other experiences featuring light seem to occur frequently around the time of a death, though they are not limited to such occasions. One woman, on the death of her mother in hospital, saw 'a shaft of bright light sloping from above and down to her'.

The *physical* sensation of an angelic presence has been felt by 9% of respondents. Some describe it as a feeling of having been 'touched by an angel', as will be addressed in a later chapter of that name. More technically, this could be called an encounter of the third kind – though this type of terminology is used more usually in connection with alien encounters, it can also be used to allude to encounters with other extraterrestrial beings. An encounter of the first kind is a visual experience – simply witnessing something as a vision or hallucination. An encounter of the second kind is characterised by communication, be it internally or externally audible, or via ESP. An encounter of the third kind occurs when there is physical contact (such as a feeling or touch) with an otherworldly being. The rarest of all is an encounter of the fourth kind, which really only occurs in alien abductions when a sexual act is carried out.

Internal sensation accounted for 9% of people who wrote to me. In this category, it was an internal sensation alone that the respondent attributed to being angelic. Miss E. Oakes wrote with a rather unique experience that happened while she was working in her garage at home. She was struggling to find a safe place to put a pile of 70 souvenir plates belonging to the church that she had agreed to store:

> With aching arms I picked up a pile of plates when I felt myself surrounded by a *smile*. I did not see any being, but the smile guided my eyes to an old box in the corner. I opened it and surprisingly found it empty. There was a safe, strong container for the plates. The 'presence' left me feeling refreshed, optimistic and warm as though soft wings surrounded me.

A sceptic may prefer to call this a gut reaction, an inner voice (though not audible), but the feeling is usually described as being far stronger than this by the recipient. Paul Dunwell lost control of his motorbike going round a bend at 70 miles per hour in the dark. Minutes before, he had passed a red sports car (also going at speed). Paul wrote:

> All I could think of was I'd risked [the life of] the driver now that my bike lay in his path on the blind bend. Telling myself that my own idiocy had brought all of this about, I resolved [to try] to move the bike despite its weight and my hands being a bit pulped. Time was, I knew, running out... then an odd thing happened... [the car] appeared on the bend at a snail's pace, his hazard warning lights already on. He stopped there and ran to me and said 'You'll never guess what's just happened... there was a light in my car. And I was told, like there was somebody there in the car with me, and actually shown that you were lying there in the road... I was told I mustn't hit you.'

Hearing an *audible* noise indicating another presence accounts for 5% of experiences received, though others have written saying they also heard an angelic choir at the time they saw an angel, so the number is actually little higher than this figure. This type of experience varies in nature – it could be a single voice giving a message or warning; some people have recalled hearing an angelic choir, or music. Such accounts are explored further in chapter six, 'Angel Voices'.

Other attributes account for the final 10% of experiences. These consist of people attributing a ghostly or misty figure, an evil presence and so forth, to being the presence of an angel. Some people see a deceased relative who helps them, whether physically or by imparting a message; this will be explored more in chapter nine, but for the sake of categorisation, such experiences are confined to this pigeonhole. Automatic reading and writing too comes into this section. This category features people who believe that an angelic force is behind the words they are writing. Other people have written to me describing experiences that, although nothing visible or audible took place, and although they may not have felt anything at the time, they later regarded a situation bearing the signs of angelic assistance, such as the example below from Margaret Cook:

> During a holiday in Kefallonia in 1995 we were travelling with friends in a car on a very wet day through the hills, twisting and turning with sheer drops most of the way with no barriers to protect [us]. At one point our car spun around and went backwards over the edge. It travelled through dense foliage, hit an olive bush/tree, the car swung round violently and was left on its side in this bush. Rescuers came rushing to our aid and we all got out safely. When we had scrambled to the top and looked down, we had missed a huge rock by only feet and the bush that stopped us travelling to the bottom of the hill was the only bush on that part of the slope. I am definitely convinced that I have a guardian angel rather than being just very, very lucky!

Note

All of the accounts and quotes listed in this book were sent to me by people who believed their experience was angelic. To the reader it is easy to try and explain such experiences away – that it was a mere coincidence or an hallucination, a gut reaction or an inner feeling. Admittedly, I have read scores of books outlining people's encounters, be they with angels, Jesus, the Blessed Virgin Mary or aliens, and at times have put the book down, quick to dismiss the stories as fantasies. But what is important here is that the people who had the experience believe with a great amount of conviction that the events as they describe them are exactly what happened: 'This sighting was not a flimsy vision. It was definitely there, more concrete than this paper you are holding.'

We were not there at the time of the experience – we are merely reading a report of something that happened, be it last week or half a century ago. Try not to judge – remember, all the accounts are from people who attributed the experience to being angelic. That is all that matters – not what I think, or you, the reader, thinks.

It is very easy for one to become preoccupied with whether or not the experience actually happened or whether it was a misinterpretation by the recipient. Perhaps a trick of the light, an obliterated reflection or maybe merely a daydream could explain the experience. The issue of the 'truth' – whether angels are 'real' – and what I believe is constantly brought up during conversations about this topic, be it from peers, journalists or respondents to the work. All I can say is I sincerely believe that all the people who have written to me believe they saw what they have described. The 'truth' doesn't enter into the equation. We go back to the question what is 'the truth' or indeed 'reality' – a book in itself! What I am interested in, as I said in the introduction, is why angels and why now? What I can assure you is that everything I have quoted is word for word taken from the letters I have received. I did not want to edit the letters or re-word them – I strongly felt that they are best left as first-hand accounts.

So, after looking at the various angelic forms and appearances that people have described seeing, let us now read in detail about such experiences.

TOUCHED BY
AN ANGEL

'... *a hand from behind grabbed the shoulder of her*
coat and physically lifted her back and up, setting
her back on the pavement [...] *at the same instant,*
a low sports car, which was travelling very fast and
she had neither seen nor heard, swept around the cor-
ner and [...] *over the exact place she had reached.*
Ella said, "I turned round still shaking, to thank the
man who dragged me back, but there was not a soul
to be seen, neither was there anyone in either direction
along the street"'

An angel's touch

On Sunday June 2 1996, a young woman presented herself for baptism during the monthly family service in a small 14th-century English village church. She had recently visited the village and attended church services there, and was so charmed by the atmosphere, and the friendliness of the people, that she and her fiancé were planning to buy a house and settle there after their marriage.

She stood beside the rector at the baptismal font towards the back of the church, accompanied only by her fiancé. When the rector began the ritual, an angel appeared at her side, placing his hand on her shoulder. He (for this angel seemed to be masculine) was tall and wore, in the words of the rector, 'something long, like a robe, but it was so white and shimmering it was almost transparent'. The angel turned his head and looked at people individually. The rector described how he was 'struck dumb, transfixed' and had trouble continuing with the ceremony. 'The three participants and the people sitting nearest them felt a tremendous electrifying energy, and during the days which followed, when they came to talk over the happening' almost all described feeling a sensation as though 'warm oil were being poured over them'. Those in the front of the church would have had to swivel around in order to witness what was happening behind them, thus those who saw the angel were mostly worshippers in the back pews near the font who had turned round specially to witness the baptism.

Among them was a woman whom I shall call Caroline, who fell into something approximating a fit. The noise and commotion caused by her falling was the first indication for the majority of the congregation that something unusual had taken place. The church warden and the rector's wife revived the woman and helped her out into the churchyard. Not knowing what to do, the church warden was told, by an angel, not to call an ambulance but to lay her down and pray. After he did so, the woman almost immediately came around declaring herself transformed, vowing to devote her life to Jesus; moreover, although she was a Roman Catholic, she insisted upon being baptised immediately. So the rector led her back into the church and performed the ceremony.

Whilst the rector, the church warden and Caroline were happy to discuss the experience with me, all were adamant that I promise to keep the participants and the name of the church unidentifiable. One of them explained: 'We don't want all sorts of weirdos turning up and people coming to see what they could see... we know we were incredibly privileged that morning and we don't want to commercialise it.'

The notion of being touched by an angel is apparently common – though the sensations differ from experience to experience, person to person. As this chapter will outline, types of experience vary considerably, from angelic smiles, to being enveloped by light or wings to being confronted by a force that saves the person from certain death or danger. All the recipients have in common the feeling that they have in some way had physical contact with something angelic. One respondent, a retired medial doctor named Dr Ernst, told me that he has often felt as if something or someone is holding his left hand – this has happened outside, in the car, at home – rather akin to the sensation of wind whistling past the hand. Like many others who claim to have had close contact with angels, he justifies himself, quick to point out that he certainly 'doesn't suffer from any neurological disorder', which of course would be the first argument from the sceptics. We discussed the fact that people today do need reason and logic in their

47

lives – but as he pointed out, some things, at times, do seemingly defy all explanation.

Other experiences seem to provide inner strength – one lady who was in an abusive relationship had reached a point at which she was periodically crying alone. On one such occasion she cried out 'Please someone help me!' and then felt a physical force – like strength – going through her body and the feeling of a hand on her shoulder and she felt calmed. From that moment on she realised she had to get out of the relationship – it took her six months, but she knew there was someone there watching over her, giving her that extra bit of inner strength.

A similar tactile experience happened to Margaret Wyartt after her son was fatally injured whilst taking part in a motor-cross event:

> At his funeral… friends prayed both before and during the service for God's love to be all around me. I was astounded by my strength and… as I sang with all my heart an angel stroked my cheek – maybe to comfort me? All I know was [I had] the feeling of three strokes and looking out of the window of the church and knowing God's love all around me.

Dee Iberson is a healer and group leader for healing and meditation. She told me '… we always invite the angels into our circle – they stand behind us with wings extended so no unwanted influences or entity can get through. It is essential to invite them, they love to be asked and stand patiently waiting for the invite. One of my group felt her angel's wings behind her and mentally asked for a hug and was delighted to feel enfolded in a loving hug.'

Experiences such as this are often the most emotional – not only does the person witness an angel, they also physically touch them or contact is made in some other way. To others, there is no vision; they simply experience the physical sensation that someone is there: 'I was very depressed on my first night as a patient with pneumonia, when an arm was put around my shoulder and I could feel a hand on my left shoulder. I couldn't see anyone there, but the experience was a great comfort to me as I knew I wasn't alone.'

A force on the roads

The concept of a 'force' either lifting, pulling, pushing or restricting movement, has been a clear thread throughout the following life-saving experiences, especially on the roads. Many respondents reported the experience of waiting to cross at the roadside and being suddenly and unexpectedly prevented from crossing. The person turns round to an empty street, with no one in sight – but soon realise that had they have crossed at that moment, they would have been knocked down. Such an account was recounted to me by a pastor who described himself as very much 'feet on the ground... and the type of person who refuses to make silly claims publicly which are no more than sensation...'

> The... incident concerned a most level-headed, elegant lady called Ella. Ella was in her late sixties when I went to [work as a priest in] Gloucester, [she was] a most beautiful pianist and church musician. It was because of my growing interest in angels that I spoke on the subject one Sunday morning. At the end of the sermon, Ella came and asked if she could speak and give a testimony.
>
> She spoke of a walk from her house into the city that took her across or beside Gloucester Park. She said [that] she was always very careful when she crossed the

road and stood carefully at the corner of a side road to check both ways. She said [on one occasion after checking and seeing nothing] she stepped off the pavement. She said that before she could take another step a hand from behind grabbed the shoulder of her coat and physically lifted her back and up, setting her back on the pavement. She said that at the same instant, a low car, which was travelling very fast and she had neither seen nor heard, swept around the corner and of course over the exact place she had reached. Ella said, 'I turned round still shaking, to thank the man who dragged me back, but there was not a soul to be seen, neither was there anyone in either direction along the street'. [Ella said] that it had to be someone big, because while she was not a heavy lady she was quite tall. Her point was that she had been lifted up and then back.

A similar story was recounted to me as follows:

I became a secretary in the city and worked in a merchant bank in Threadneedle Street. I crossed the road one day forgetting that the one way system had been changed to two way, and therefore only looked to the right. Halfway across the road I met a strong force stopping me going any further and a car drove past me from the left. I should most certainly have been killed if that unseen force hadn't stopped me.

A Mrs Hambley came up against a similar unseen barrier back in 1956 when she was a 14-year-old schoolgirl. It was a dark and wintry evening and with a friend and her mother they awaited the departure of their bus to take them home.

Suddenly Mrs Collins realised she had left her bag at the

nearby Wharf Café and asked Lesley to fetch it for her. The bus was due to leave and my friend's mother becomes anxious.

I offered to go and help Lesley find the bag, and rushed from the bus; confused by the mixture of dazzling lights and darkness I headed straight towards a fire engine hurtling past. Was it shock reaction or, as I believe, [was I] held back on either side and protected in front by an invisible wall? I was bewildered and somewhat shaken by the experience but grateful to have survived.

The following account of a preventative force comes from Jim D'Eath, though his experience differs in the sense that the preventative force was dispelled from a frail elderly lady who came and stood beside him as he was waiting to cross the road.

I used to walk from home to my office every work day at the same time and by the same route for several years, so I was used to passing the same people. One morning, however, I was waiting to cross the road with an old lady whom I had never noticed before. As I stepped off the curb a car appeared which I had not seen and at that moment I felt this old lady's arm restrain me across my chest, thereby preventing me from taking a further step in front of this oncoming car.

The car passed and I glanced at the old lady in thanks before crossing the road. When I reached the other side I looked to see if she had followed me across but she was nowhere to be seen. I then realised how close I had come to a major accident through lack of concentration and had a strong feeling that the timely intervention had been angelic and there was no other explanation...

Pushed from danger

Other people have shared with me their experiences of being pushed by some force out of danger. Richard Watkins was climbing Ben Levi in Perthshire back in the 1970s via a steep route. Instead of sticking to the gully he had started up, he moved out onto the more open, exposed hillside, which proved even more risky. 'As I neared the top,' he wrote, 'I was trembling with fear yet I felt a sort of force beaming me up, ensuring that I reached the top of the rocky section safely. There was no sense of any personal angel or other being – just this kindly protective assistance.'

Another dramatic account occurred back in 1929, when Father Augustine Hoey, then aged 14, had gone on holiday with a friend's family to Filey. He decided to climb some very steep cliffs, despite seeing a memorial stone marking the fate of a boy who had fallen into the sea whilst climbing the cliffs, drowning. Undaunted, he began to climb the cliffs – only to become stuck. With crashing waves below him and an overhang above, he became rigid with fear, scared to move in case he too fell to his death. Then the clump of grass he was grasping began to give way. He froze with fear. Suddenly he felt himself being pushed up by what can only be described as a mighty force; he was pushed until he lay, gasping for breath on the grassy cliff top above.

A similar foolhardy slip happened to Peter Dyke, who was five years old at the time:

> On this particular day my parents had taken me to Portland Bill. After being cooped up in the car for a long journey I was really pleased to get out and explore the cliffs. The cliffs are rather unusual as they have a flat cap of stone rather like a table and this flat

top has fissures running through it, around seventy foot straight down I would guess, and they are open to the sea, so waves surge up them at high water. One of these fissures was to nearly be my downfall. I had slipped away from my parents and was running around rather stupidly and not looking where I was going. I saw the gap, realised I could not stop and jumped. I didn't think I would make it, however, as I crossed the gap I felt as though I was given a shove or maybe more support – as I recall It was a bit like going over a humped-back bridge – only I could not say how I was held. It was like being weightless, only not (I am so sorry – that is the best way I can describe it!). I can remember looking down the gap and seeing the sea below – I will never forget that! By the way, we are not talking Peter Pan-type flying here – the gap was only a bit further than I could jump. When I was on the other side I looked round rather quickly, largely in the hope that Mum and Dad had not seen what I had just done! As I looked round I saw... I was going to say [a] figure but I don't think it was... I think [a] 'form' would be more appropriate – definitely faceless, no wings and coloured rather like smoked glass. As I saw it, so it disappeared although it was barely there to start with – rather like a heat haze over a really hot fire.

Another 'force' saved art gallery owner Dena Bryant-Duncan. It was getting dark, the day before Christmas Eve, and her accountant called to collect some framing from Dena's husband and some paintings that she had bought as Christmas presents.

She had put her car outside the gallery, which was on a small crossroads. All the streets were tiny and winding near the abbey, and no one seemed to know the right of way. As my husband put the pictures in the car for her we stood chatting, one on each side of the shop steps. Because it had been a cottage many years ago, there were two quite steep steps in front of the door. As we talked and laughed there was suddenly a terrific metallic grinding noise and a crash. As we looked, two cars had crashed into each other on the small crossroad, and were heading straight at me. I was rooted to the spot. I am a disabled person and not able to move quickly, but I was totally unable to move at all. I knew I was about to be killed.

'God my poor family, and at Christmas too!' I prayed. Suddenly I felt myself wafted up those two steep steps, and gently deposited inside the shop. I did not feel hands under me, only feathery wings.

There was a huge crash as one car hit the wall in the exact spot where I had been standing only seconds previously. I am quite sure my guardian angel saved me. It took quite a time [for the] ambulances and police to deal with the situation, not to mention my poor accountant, who was in a state of shock and I had to see to her. Nothing could be done that night. The police put cones round the car, [which was] embedded in my wall and obstructing the pavement. The next day, as [a] young man winched the car up on to his breakdown trolley he called out, 'Wonderful these old buildings, ain't they?' There was not a mark or a scratch where the vehicle had crashed into my wall. Yet the car was a complete write-off. I am sure my guardian angel saved me. And I was able to have a wonderful Christmas with my three sons.

Another 'force' aided Rosalin McCullough quite recently. Rosalin had sold her home and was staying with one of her daughters while she awaited the completion of her new house. During the week she often attended Mass at the little convent nearby. One Thursday she was on the way when she fell:

> I slipped forward with some force and was heading for a crack on the forehead, I imagine. To my surprise, I was pushed sideways onto the grass verge with an even greater force but had no injury, thank God. A woman stopped her car and said she had seen what happened and could she give me a lift? I declined and pressed on for Mass – then, at the consecration, I started sobbing as the realisation occurred to me that my angel must have pushed me sideways. I was 'moving' in ten days and I couldn't possibly have been laid up having legal documents to sign and having booked removals, etc. My faith in the angels is *well* justified.

A similar incident happened to Dorothy Nicholls several years ago. At the time, Dorothy had recently converted to Christianity and was a young mother:

> I was doing the family washing. My two toddlers were playing somewhere around the house or garden and their tricycles and other large toys lay heaped awkwardly, in a tangle of metal and plastic, at the foot of the steps by our rear door. When I was ready to peg out the washing I carried it, piled high, in a bowl or basket in front of me. It largely obscured my vision. As I came out of the door and went to walk down the steps, I was aware of a lifting sensation and seemed to float – all in just a few seconds – down the steps and

over the heap of toys. Only then did I see and realise the hazard and that I had apparently been saved from a dangerous fall...

I have always linked that experience with Psalm 91 verses 9–12 ['Because you have made the Lord your refuge, the Most High your dwelling place, no evil shall befall you, no scourge come near your tent. For he will command his angels concerning you to guard you in all your ways. On their hands they will bear you up, so that you will not dash your foot against a stone.']¹ I cannot explain why, at other times, and for other people, this removal from danger may not automatically be the case.

Enveloped by wings

In my opening chapter, Miss Oakes gave an account of feeling wrapped in what she described as an angelic smile. Other people have outlined the physical experiences of being engulfed in light, or the sensation of being hugged or enveloped by vast angel wings, as Valerie Shipley describes:

About ten years ago I was sitting quietly. I was not ill. I had nothing in particular to worry me. I was not asleep. What I saw and felt was nothing like a dream. I felt that I was looking into a cave made of sheets of blue light. I felt as if I was moving towards the cave. Then I realised it was not a cave but a winged being. What I had taken to be a cave was in fact huge wings made of sheets of blue light, like feathers. I was not moving towards it at all – in fact, it was moving towards me, to enfold me in its wings.

I heard no voice, but a strong message on what I can only call a flow of 'love'. The message was that everything is 'alright'. Everything in some way was in order and will work out all right in the end – not just for me, but everything. Everything was a part of everything else. All is one.

I have no religious faith. I had never thought about winged beings or angels before this… only this year [1998] I noticed a text in a church. It said 'All is well, all is well and all manner of things are well' (Julian of Norwich). That is more or less the message/feeling that I had.

The sensation of being enveloped by wings has also been experienced by Mrs Henry, whose 'experiences have taken place countless times over a few decades. They take [the form] of angelic wings covering my bed as a bedspread. I am aware of being totally enveloped by the presence.' Mary Miller has 'seen angels during prayer sessions when we have been asking for help for those very much in need – [for example, those who are sick]. Details of angels I cannot really remember except for these huge, feathered wings they put round people for protection.'

Angela Tillotson has also had the sensation of being engulfed, but in her case she was surrounded by pure light:

It was on the Saturday night before Palm Sunday – March 26 1994. I didn't actually see anything, but experienced a strong presence and felt (or was aware of) a 'carapace' of light wrapped around my shoulders. This was during a very difficult car journey and I was by myself and I had no doubt at the time that I was being protected by a guardian angel who duly delivered me home safely.

Sylvia Mace sent me the final experience to be listed in this category. She recalled the time in 1998 when her eight-week-old daughter was admitted to hospital with bronchiolitis complicated by a collapsed lung. Her oxygen levels were very poor even on optimum oxygenation via a headbox, and it looked as if she would need to be ventilated. As she wrote:

My husband and I were in a state of complete panic. I went to the Ladies and rested my head on the wall and prayed, 'God will you please just let me see where You are in all this because I can't tell.'

I then went back to the room where my husband and daughter were. I took my place at the opposite side of her cot to him. As I stood there, the experience I felt can only be described as being wrapped in the softest feathers, or velvet, something indescribably soft, and just being held. With it came an indescribable sense of peace, in total contrast to my feelings only seconds before. I am convinced I was being wrapped in angel wings and comforted and reassured. I looked over at my husband to smile at him, as I felt everything would be all right, and saw angels beside him.

There were two male figures, about eight feet tall standing at either side of my husband. They had shoulder-length hair, and were wearing bronze-coloured robes... They had faces which were both youthful and mature at the same time. They were both looking down on my husband as if keeping watch, and they both had their hands on swords, which were hanging in belts around their waists, as if ready for action. I then said, 'This is all very well God, but where are Nicola's angels?' My attention was then drawn to her cot, which was so bright even the figures by Martin looked dull, and the words came to me (which I later found in Deuteronomy): 'The eternal God is your refuge, and underneath are the everlasting Arms'. God was telling me that he was with Nicola, his arms were around her and He would heal.

Nicola later made a full recovery and was discharged much sooner than the staff and [my husband]... would have imagined.

SAVED!

'To describe her appearance, I would say she glows, she looks rather like a Pre-Raphaelite goddess in a Burn-Jones painting. She wears a light, long robe and a jewelled collar; she has an aquiline nose […] I could not say what colour her hair and eyes are, but they are perfect. All this really sounds like I am quite mad, but really I am not…'

THE CHRISTIAN CHURCH teaches that when a child is born, he or she is assigned a guardian angel that will watch over and protect him or her all their lives. The Talmud too speaks of every Jew being attended throughout his life by 11,000 guardian angels; also that 'every blade of grass has over it an angel saying 'grow'.' From the data collected for this project it is clear that many people, from Roman Catholics to atheists, Muslims to agnostics, Hindu to Jews, believe absolutely in angels.

I received letters from young mothers stating that their babies have had guardians watching over them, some of which they could see. Heather Simmons, for example, was aware of a presence she believed to be an angel around each of her babies in their earliest months. 'The reason I think they were angels is because [they were] good, calm, peaceful and amused the babies. [They were] up high, above my shoulders or head, near the ceiling. There was nothing else in [the babies'] eyeline, such as a light, and they would look at this nothingness for ages. I am a firm believer in presences not seen or felt by all. Perhaps babies or children have heightened awareness or sensitivity to them.'

It is also apparent that the belief deceased relatives come back as guardian angels is common – this will be explored further in chapter nine, 'Angels of Death'. One lady told me her guardian was either her grandfather himself, who died whilst she was very young, or is somehow connected with him. Often she feels something prevents her from doing things, only later to realise by following this 'feeling' it was the right thing to do. This instantaneous gut reaction is often attributed to angelic inspiration or intervention. Margaret Cook wrote about a time she was crossing the road on a pelican crossing where the traffic had halted:

> I was halfway across when I was compelled to look right and coming up and the outside was a car out of control, which sped past me with just millimetres to spare.

We have all heard stories from others, even if we have not had such experiences personally, in which the inexplicable has happened. These make take the form of having an instinct not to travel somewhere by car and hearing there was a pile up on the route that would have been taken, or being aided by a stranger or a presence in a dangerous or threatening situation, right down to coincidences so great they prevented what could otherwise have been fatal accidents.

The perfect stranger: companionship in threatening situations

Caroline Plant was on her way to the opera and decided to take an unfamiliar route. She soon realised she'd made a bad decision – the subway she ended up at used to be known as the 'Bullring' and is notoriously unsafe – winos and tramps frequent the area and Caroline began to pray she would make it to the Tube station safely. However, almost out of nowhere a tall, pale woman appeared wearing a long tweed coat – Caroline began to walk faster to try and catch up with her. Halfway through the subway the atmosphere became really menacing, and at one point a drunken man leered out toward her. She braced herself as he got closer, but even though he was just a few feet away, he simply stared straight through both her and the second woman as if they weren't there. The beggars who were sitting in the tunnel didn't seem to notice them either; no one hassled the pair for money or flinched as they walked by. They wound round passages and through roads, the woman walking the same route Caroline had planned for herself. As they reached the metal steps of the Tube she could hear the footsteps of the woman ascending – Caroline called to her, something to the effect of 'Thanks – safety in numbers, eh?' and followed up the metal stairs a few steps behind her. However, at the top the woman had disappeared – she was nowhere to be seen along the whole length of the concourse. Caroline insists that her companion couldn't possibly have walked out of sight in such a short space of time.

Another helpful presence came to the aid of Daphne Pink. Daphne was in her early twenties at the time and a friend of hers was in hospital, having just had a baby:

> Her husband wanted to visit her but was looking after his three children. I said I would babysit for him so he could visit. My husband was looking after our small child so I had to walk there. All was well and after my friend's husband returned he told me all the news. I wasn't looking forward to the walk home as it was a very dark area to be in but I knew it had to be done as he couldn't leave three children on their own... as I was walking home, scared stiff, in the middle of a road of houses, I suddenly saw a tall man in a hacking jacket and trousers in front of me... I was about twenty paces behind and I felt comforted knowing I wasn't alone. As I got to the end of the road, the man vanished – he could not possibly have gone into a house and I suddenly realised there had been no footsteps [coming from him]. I now believe he had been sent to keep me company on the way home.

When Jean Freeman was 15 years old, back in 1949, she

moved house and had to travel to school in the opposite direction to commuters, so subsequently her trains were comparatively empty:

In those days we had what we called Watford trains, i.e. brown coaches with contained carriages and no connecting corridors, and Uxbridge trains that were red through-carriage underground trains. Unaware of the perils, I got on a Watford train one morning and found myself alone with a man of about thirty-five in the opposite corner. I got out a book to read as I always did, but when we left Wembley Park Station he moved and came and sat opposite me, leaning forward and talking. Fear gripped me, but I kept reading and ignored him and noticed that the door handle was in my favour, being near to my left hand. I decided to block it with my knee at the next station so that he couldn't stop me opening the door and leaping out. The next station, Preston Road was only a short distance away, but I knew the one after that was much farther and he might start something then. As the train arrived at Preston Road I looked out of the window to judge when I should start opening the door when I saw a lady rushing down the steps with a small boy. She was looking at the train most intently, but as my carriage was at the front and she was obviously only just in time to catch the train it never occurred to me she would come right to the front of the train. Nevertheless, she did and got into my carriage. The man looked annoyed and sat back, and the relief I felt was wonderful. I had never seen the woman and the boy together before, nor since. After that I always caught the Uxbridge train!

A similar experience happened to Vanessa Lillingston-Price while she was in America in 1986:

> I was waiting at a bus stop – standing on crutches as a I'd had an operation on my leg – when a homeless, drunken [man] began harassing me. I obviously couldn't move away from him – or walk easily to the next stop. As his language became more threatening and suggestive, I began to pray in earnest because I was afraid and needed, as I said to God, a knight in shining armour on a charger to come and rescue me!
>
> Moments later, an amazing black sports car pulled up on the opposite side of the road, unique in design, sleek and shiny. The dark, tinted window rolled down and a fair-skinned, blond man leaned out and shouted 'Oi! You! Leave her alone!' The man who'd been harassing me stumbled into the road and walked towards the car where upon the angel (?) rolled the window up and drove off – the drunk stumbling along behind as if transfixed.

Vanessa added, 'I kept hoping the driver would return to give me a lift home but sadly he never did! Whether he was a mere mortal of the Lord or an angel taking on human form, I have no idea. But I have never forgotten him – nor cease to smile when I remember God's Knights of the Eighties with their sleek cars instead of chargers!'

Vanessa experienced another close scrape with danger in Pakistan. She'd been travelling in the northern region on holiday with two girlfriends and a man they had persuaded to join them for safety. They were staying in Gilgit and had grown more at ease about the area, believing the nationals to be familiar with foreigners and friendly towards them.

Perhaps we'd become almost too relaxed our last night, as we left the company of our male chaperone to walk back through the town and down an unlit track towards the hotel.

Walking down this track we were amazed by how dark it had become, so that you couldn't see very far ahead... suddenly we were aware of sinister male voices behind us. We picked up the pace of our walk and began praying – at first asking forgiveness for our foolishness [at leaving] our chaperone and [taking] this unlit route, and then, as our fears rose, merely repeating the Lord's Prayer. The voices grew in number and seemed to get closer.

We turned a corner in the road and were suddenly confronted by a huge beam of light which enveloped us and appeared almost solid in the surrounding blackness, and dazzling. We continued towards the source and relaxed as the sinister voices slunk back into the darkness.

Just as suddenly as it appeared, the light disappeared. We never found the source or the person who [could] have directed it. There were no streetlights at that point and certainly not the technology to produce a floodlight out of nowhere in that particular area. We continued in safety and amazement at this coincidence until we neared the hotel and streetlights appeared again. At this juncture a young boy ran up from behind and pinched my friend's bottom before running off again! It came to us as a lesson not to repeat the same error in future and maintain the same standards of behaviour and culture as our national counterparts.

Dr John Burch felt the presence of an angel back in November

1996 while walking his dog along a canal path. It was a wintry evening, exceptionally forbidding and bleak. 'It was very dark by the canal and I was frightened, what of I don't know, as I was walking down the slope to the tow path,' John revealed. He prayed for protection and to his surprise saw an eight-foot angel wearing a white robe and with wings folded behind. 'He glowed, he was white, his hair was white and I got the impression in my mind that he was a guardian angel. I think God put that impression in my mind but what he was really showing me was that this angel was there to protect me from harm.'[2] He went on to say, 'I could see the top joint of the wing level with the angel's shoulder and could see the feathers on the wings. The face was without expression, but was benign. The eyes were not looking at me but behind and beyond me. The strong message that I received was that I need have no fear because my guardian angel was always on duty to protect me.'

Gillian Burton has always been wary of accidents while travelling, after her family was involved in a car crash:

I was flying back from Aberdeen with my husband on a very windy day. Just before setting off I saw a white shadowy figure squatting in the empty space in front of the emergency exit. He was wearing a long white gown, Eastern style, and had no wings... seeing him was a huge comfort and I felt very safe even though when in the air, the plane was buffeted along by the wind. We arrived early above the airport and had to go into a stack – five minutes in a spiral going up; awaiting permission to land; then five minutes going down again. It was only after we landed safely [that I thanked] this figure. I knew he would then disappear, and he did. Someone later explained it was probably an angel and I believe they were probably right.

Like Gillian, many people wrote to me talking about feeling a presence of something that they can only describe as being their guardian angel, which is with them whenever they travel. Bridget wrote:

> I am utterly convinced that I have a guardian angel. [She] has been with me all my life, but has made her presence known to me more strongly in recent years... my guardian angel is something I have never ever discussed with a living soul, for fear of ridicule – at [best] I would be thought eccentric, at worst a raving lunatic!
>
> ... She travels with me in my car when I undertake long journeys and I feel safe; she walks with me when I have to go out at night, and I am protected. When I am troubled or worried, her slogan is 'All will be well' and I am comforted.
>
> To describe her appearance, I would say she glows, she looks rather like a Pre-Raphaelite goddess in a Burn-Jones painting. She wears a light, long robe and a jewelled collar, she has an aquiline nose; [...] I could not say what colour her hair and eyes are, but they are perfect. All this really sounds like I am quite mad, but really I am not...'

Peg wrote of her guardian angels: 'I have felt the presence of something outside my own intelligence. I can't see them or touch them, but "they" – a group – are so near to me that I can almost feel the feathers of their wings.'

As we have seen, in some cases angels appeared to remove not the actual danger, but rather the fear of it. One of the most poignant vignettes from World War I is the well-documented tale of the angel of Mons from the Battle of the Somme in

August 1914. It is alleged that as wounded soldiers were taken to field hospitals they individually began reporting to nurses that they had seen angels on the field. The French saw the Archangel Michael, riding a white horse. The British said it was Saint George, 'a tall man with yellow hair in golden armour, on a white horse, holding his sword up, and his mouth open, crying "Victory."'[3] The nurses reported a startling serenity in the dying men, as though they had nothing to fear.

Through the subsequent decades, there has been much speculation regarding these accounts – they have been put down to hallucinations brought on by exhaustion, or simply mass hysteria. However, it was later found that stories had emerged from the German side of the same incident. The Kaiser's soldiers said they found themselves 'absolutely powerless to proceed... and their horses turned around sharply and fled'.[4] The Germans said the allied position was held by thousands of Allied troops, though in fact there were only two regiments there.

A mass of material exists that attempts to discredit the theory of mass apparition of angels at Mons. However, many of the accounts are so dramatic that I believe something extraordinary must have happened that night, whether it was brought about by the presence of angels or by something else. Joyce Trott spoke to me about her father's experiences at that battle:

My father won a military medal during that battle – how he won it I'll never know, because he said it was too terrible to talk about. There were about sixty thousand who went out to fight this battle and he [told me] 'We were down to about thirty odd thousand... I can not give you the exact figures but... we were more than half left and the battle was getting impossible because the Germans had bigger and better equipment than [us].' He said he'd never experienced anything like it – they were dropping down like flies and all of a sudden, [there] was an eerie sound and there was a white light across the hill and they saw these crowds on horses riding across the top of the hill. The Germans kept firing for a while but all of a sudden gave up. He said they'd never seen anybody run as fast as these Germans over the hill and he [told me], 'We were all awe-inspired and we looked up and said someone was doing some work.' He said to me, 'Always be a Christian and believe in the Lord, because he saved us that day through the angels.'[5]

Close shaves

Near misses that almost proved fatal are, of course, common, and sceptics can quickly explain them away as coincidence or luck – but some of the accounts I received from people who told me how they narrowly escaped death do stand out. Having survived his moment of trauma at the Filey cliffs experience, Fr. Augustine Hoey had a similar brush with fate one evening in 1944 whilst he was serving as an assistant priest during the war. He heard the familiar buzz of a falling bomb and as the air-raid sirens begin to wail he asked the lady whom he was instructing for confirmation whether they should all take shelter – they agreed not to, as the situation was so familiar. The next thing he remembers is being dragged from the debris, sustaining just a small cut. Everyone else had died. Devastation was everywhere.

Fr. Hoey experienced yet another close shave some years later in 1952, whilst he was preaching in a packed church at a colliery in South Yorkshire. A large coping stone from one of the pillars came hurtling down, missing his face by inches and landing in the only available tiny space, free of people. I also received a report of a very similar experience that occurred more recently: a lady walked out of her flat during the great storms of 1987 when there was a terrific crash right behind her. She turned around to see that a huge ridge tile from the roof had fallen and shattered centimetres from where she had previously been standing.

Michael Batterham, a retired army officer, has had two memorable brushes with fate. The first took place in 1983 whilst he was on holiday in Bude, north Cornwall:

> Being then fifty-three and still a reasonably strong swimmer, I enjoyed the sea and surf. We always took our surfboards on holiday (not the expert stand-up type, but the lie-down ones). Most people picked up a wave about fifty yards out to sea and surfed into the shallows. Being bold and a bit foolhardy I liked to go out a bit further than the rest. I remember being about thirty yards further [out], possibly more, and there being no one anywhere near me. The water was probably about chest high. I suddenly realised that I was not moving towards the shore but away [from it] and swimming did not help. I had probably got into a rip current. Obviously I began to panic and waved to the lifeguards, who were some distance away on the top of the cliff and my signal was acknowledged. At that moment a man appeared beside me with a surfboard; not the wooden type, which most adults use, but a polystyrene one used by children and beginners. These float, but the wooden ones do not. He told me to hold on to the board and pushed me into the shore. As we reached the shore, I noticed the lifeguard running towards me. Naturally, my first action was to turn and thank the man who had rescued me. He was nowhere to be seen. I believe he

was an angel, but at the time I was too shocked to share the experience, even with my family, and even since have told it to only a few.

His second eerie experience occurred in September 1997:

At about 7.45 p.m. I was driving my Peugeot 205 alone to the church prayer meeting, which was about three miles from my home... I have done this journey many times in the nineteen years I have attended my church. Although [it's] a thirty-mile-per-hour limit, most people get up speed going downhill to get up the other side easily, so my speed was probably forty miles per hour. Near the bottom of the hill I noticed a Ford Transit van coming towards me, travelling fast, at about the same distance from the bottom of the hill as me. Suddenly he swerved wildly across the road in front of me (I learnt later he had had a blow-out). Assuming his speed was also forty miles per hour, though it could have been more, our combined approach speed was eighty miles per hour. I estimate our distance apart was thirty to forty yards. I calculate that I had one second before impact, not time even for an arrow prayer!

I remember nothing of that second, but pulled into a small road junction, put my flashers on and got out to see if the other driver was OK. I looked round and his van was reversed into the bank about fifty yards up the hill I had just driven down! The driver was on his mobile phone and not hurt. I said something like, 'That was a near one.' And he replied 'Yes, but I missed you!' He said he was alright so I went on to the meeting... you may think that this was an example of

God's protection of His own, but I believe someone
other than the driver must have been in that van!

Miraculous escapes

I think we would all agree that evidence from adults is easily
open to challenge, but when it comes from a small child,
credibility can take on a new meaning. Children are incredibly
open, fresh and aware. They have not yet learnt to be sceptical
and do not realise people may disbelieve them or perhaps
laugh at what they report seeing, as they talk have no preconceptions or worries about the words they choose to
describe what they see. I do believe that, in some ways,
accounts from children tend to add greater validity to the
claims for the existence of angels. After all, kids say what they
see – they do not share the unfortunate inhibitions and taboos
we learn later in our adult life.[6]

Judith Shrimpton, a G.P., was a witness to something that
seems to defy the comprehension of eye witnesses and medical
evidence.

It was nearly forty years ago and I was working as a
third-year medical student in the casualty department
of St. Mary's Hospital, Paddington. I was an atheist, a
typical student of the time, and working with me was
another student, [called] Jenny. Anyone less fanciful
than Jenny is hard to imagine. She was a healthy,
hearty woman who had played lacrosse for Roedean.

A young child was brought in on a stretcher. She
was unconscious and accompanied by her very
distressed parents, a policeman, and a bystander at the
time. Lucy had run into the middle of the busy
Edgware Road and a lorry had hit her and then the
wheels had gone over her – not just once but twice –

74

the rear as well. The policeman who had been on duty had watched it happen.

Together with the doctor on duty, the three of us examined the unconscious child. Apart from one small bruise on her shoulder she was totally unmarked. We were about to send her off for X-rays, when she opened her eyes and smiled. 'Where is that man in white?' she demanded. The doctor came forward. 'No – no,' said Lucy, 'the man in the long shiny dress.' We held her hands and stroked her face. 'The man did that,' said Lucy, 'he stroked my face, as he picked up the wheels' – 'the wheels did not touch me,' she added.

Lucy then fell into a totally normal, deep sleep. A full medical examination revealed not a single injury, except for the small bruise. The following day, Lucy was discharged. The lorry driver swore that he had felt two bumps and had vomited in the road at the sight of the unconscious Lucy. Lucy herself retained a child's quiet unconcern and certainty that 'the man in white had lifted the lorry'.

Although not included in this research as it is not from the UK, the following account has been distributed widely across the internet and has been sent to me many times. It follows closely on from Lucy's miraculous escape and has been hard to edit down. I hope the flavour of it has not been lost in doing so.

Three-year-old Brian had been revived after becoming trapped for several minutes underneath an automatic garage door that had crushed his sternum above his heart. After endless surgery over the next month, Brian awoke from an afternoon nap. The following is in the words of his father, Lloyd Glenn. I have tried to contact Lloyd, but without any luck. I would love to talk to him about his experiences, and I hope he doesn't mind me reproducing his story here.

'Sit down, Mommy, I have something to tell you.' At this time in his life, Brian usually spoke in small phrases, so to say a large sentence surprised my wife. She sat down with him on his bed and he began his sacred and remarkable story.

'Do you remember when I got stuck under the garage door? Well, it was so heavy and it hurt really bad. I called to you, but you couldn't hear me. I started to cry, but then it hurt too bad. And then the 'birdies' came.'

'The birdies?' my wife asked, puzzled.

'Yes,' he replied. 'The 'birdies' made a whooshing sound and flew into the garage. They took care of me.'

'They did?'

'Yes, he said.' 'One of the birdies came and got you and she came to tell you I got stuck under the door.' My wife realised that a three-year-old had no concept of death and spirits, so he was referring to the beings who came to him from beyond as 'birdies' because they were up in the air like birds that fly.

'What did the birdies look like?' she asked.

Brian answered. 'They were so beautiful. They were dressed in white – all white. Some of them had green and white. But some of them had on just white.'

'Did they say anything?'

'Yes,' he answered. 'They told me the baby would be all right.'

'What baby?'

And Brian answered, 'The baby laying on the garage floor.' He went on, 'You came out and opened the garage door and ran to the baby. You told the baby to stay and not leave.'

My wife nearly collapsed upon hearing this, for she had indeed gone and knelt beside Brian's body and seeing his crushed chest and unrecognisable features, knowing he was already dead, she looked up around her and whispered, 'Don't leave us Brian, please stay if you can.'

As she listened to Brian telling her the words she had spoken, she realised that the spirit had left his body and was looking down from above. 'Then what happened?' she asked.

'We went on a trip, far, far away...' He grew agitated trying to say the things he didn't seem to have the words for. My wife tried to calm him and comfort him, and let him know it would be okay. He struggled with wanting to tell something that was obviously very important to him, but finding the words was difficult.

'We flew so fast up in the air. They're so pretty, Mommy,' he added. 'And there is lots and lots of birdies.'

Brian went on to tell her that the 'birdies' had told him that he had to come back and tell everyone about the 'birdies'. He said they brought him back to the house, and that a big fire truck and an ambulance were there. A man was bringing the baby out on a white bed and he tried to tell the man the baby would be okay, but the man couldn't hear him. He said, 'Birdies told him he had to go with the ambulance, but they would be near him.' They were so pretty and peaceful, he didn't want to come back. And then the bright light came. He said the light was so bright and so

warm and he loved the bright light so much. Someone
was in the bright light and put their arms around him
and told him, 'I love you but you have to go back. You
have to play baseball, and tell everyone about the
birdies.' Then the person in the bright light kissed him
and waved bye-bye. Then whoosh, the big sound
came and they went into the clouds.

The story went on for an hour. He told us, 'The
birdies [are] always with us, but we don't see them
because we look with our eyes and we don't hear
them because we listen with our ears. But they are
always there, you can only see them in here (and he
put his hand over his heart). They whisper the things
to help us do what is right because they love us so
much.' Brian continued, stating 'I have a plan,
Mommy. You have a plan. Daddy has a plan.
Everyone has a plan. We must all live our plan and
keep our promises. The birdies help us to do that
because they love us all so much.'

In the weeks that followed, he often came to us
and told all, or part of it, again and again. Always the
story remained the same. The details were never
changed or out of order. A few times he added further
bits of information and clarified the message he had
already delivered. It never ceased to amaze us how he
could tell such detail and speak beyond his ability
when he spoke of his 'birdies'.

Everywhere he went, he told complete strangers
about the 'birdies'. No one ever looked at him
strangely when he did this. Rather, they always [got] a
profound, softened look on their face and [smiled].
Needless to say, we have not been the same ever since
that day, and I pray we never will be.

A HELPING HAND

*'All of a sudden a lady dressed in bright blue
appeared with blonde hair tied up on top. She smiled
at me and said 'You're in trouble aren't you?' and
handed me four tickets for the family. My husband
George was amazed. We looked up to thank her but
she had disappeared.'*

I WAS PROBABLY about eight and my sister five. I went out with my sister in the pushchair accompanied by my friend Peter, my mother having forbidden me to go near the canal. We ended up on the canal towpath. Peter and I wanted to investigate the ground up a side bank and I told my sister to stay in the pushchair. She didn't, she started following us up the slope pulling the pushchair which she let go of and it ran down into the water!

Not only had I disobeyed my mother, but had lost the pushchair, my coat and hat too. I started crying and prayed for help when all of a sudden this boy came down the slope with a scaffold-type pole with a curved end and he quickly had the pushchair, coat and hat retrieved from the canal.

I remember at the time thinking it was a miracle rather than a coincidence and I am still convinced to this day that this boy with the pole was somebody rather special – perhaps an angel.

Not all angelic experiences are life-saving or preventative instances. The following accounts, although similar to those featured in the previous chapter, contain far less dramatic angels – manifestations that are, in a word, more mundane. Here they seemingly take on roles to assist with more menial tasks. In none of these accounts was the recipient in crisis, ill or seeking an experience. They occurred, so it seemed out of the blue, to simply offer a helping hand in a person's hour of need.

I have had countless accounts from people who experienced perilous moments connected with their cars. The following accounts are prime examples of cars that had become well and truly stuck, be it in a ditch, in heavy snow or mud. In all cases, someone 'appeared' seemingly out of nowhere, helped the person in distress, and then disappeared.

About 40 years ago, Yvette Dalal, her brother and another friend, decided to drive straight down the Iberian Peninsula from Vittoria, through Madrid and onto Toledo, thence to Gibraltar. Yvette takes up the story:

> We were all in our early twenties, in our first jobs after being students and very optimistic about life. Interestingly. we were all agnostics, and thought we knew it all.
>
> Foolishly, we set out without a supply of food and water, in our friend's Volkswagen Beetle. After some hours we found ourselves in a kind of moonscape of red earth, rocks and dust. There were no road signs, and what road there had been had degenerated into a track between the rocks, and nothing, but nothing to indicate that anyone would be stupid enough to travel the route we had chosen. I must stress that there was nothing there – not even a derelict hut.
>
> We were in an elevated position and could see for miles around in all directions. The immensity of Spain was very evident. Having noted that the burning sun was directly overhead we set off in the direction which, we hoped, was south. Before we had gone very far the car lurched and came to a rest with the rear side wheels in a deep ditch that had been impossible to see in the blinding sunlight. We couldn't move it backwards or forwards, and it resisted all efforts to be lifted. We had no water to assuage our raging thirst, there was no one around and we were completely ignorant of our location. No mobile phones in those days! We were scared!

Then it happened. Silently, without any warning, a young man appeared as [if] from out of the rocks. Dressed in white, longish dark hair, he smiled at us, bent, put his hands under the side of the car and lifted it out of that ditch as if it were made of matchwood. We were agog – where did he come from? All he did was smile and point, then turned and walked away, disappearing into the shimmering rock-scape.

We drove in the direction indicated and eventually reached a decent road that led us to Madrid.

I have thought about him from time to time over the years – could he have been an angel?

Mrs Hickman's encounter took place back in August 1977 when she and her husband toured the Thames Valley in their brand new two-week-old car:

The morning dawned – fairly damp, but as we were to join our daughters in Wales later that day, we carried on undaunted by the weather. Rain, rain and more rain. We travelled around looking for the Vale of the White Horse, but could not find it anywhere, I think it must have got lost in the fog!

Eventually we found a track – miles from anywhere – and drove for a little while between cornfields; we could not turn the car around, there were hedges on either side. Then, calamity – the car was slowly sinking into the mud. This was our first new, beautiful car, just two weeks old. Try as we would, the car would not move, the wheels were covered in slimy mud almost to the top of the wheel arches. We were convinced that we would lose the car completely after trying everything that we possibly could, including pushing straw (found in a nearby field) under the wheels.

Suddenly from out of the mist appeared four men. Dressed in hikers' gear, with rucksacks, and drenched the same as we were, they took control. Within minutes they lifted the car, with one man at each wheel, straight out of the slimy mud and deposited it on firmer ground. We could not believe what was happening! Our kind Samaritans would not take any money to buy a drink. Our thanks seemed very feeble payment. They only spoke a few words, we turned to get back into the car, then turned again to wave a last goodbye – but they had completely disappeared. The path was at least two miles long, with fields on either side, – there was no sign of these four men.

I have always believed that we all have guardian angels, and on this occasion they were definitely with us on our holiday in the Thames Valley and especially in the Vale of the White Horse. They disappeared as quickly as they had appeared on that muddy track.

Like computers, cars are fabulous when they work, but a complete bane when something goes wrong. Many experiences have been related to me involving instances of cars breaking down in the middle of nowhere only for assistance to arrive miraculously. Consider the following account from Janet Cass of an incident that occurred a few years ago:

We have a son Living in Lytham, Lancs, which is quite a journey from Essex, especially if the traffic and weather lengthen our journey time. At the time mentioned, we had been generally held up on the M6 – so what's new? – pouring rain, heavy clouds and night approaching – all making visibility rather poor.

Approaching some traffic lights on the last leg of our tiring trip, somewhere near Preston, the car died on us and wouldn't start again. Cars behind us had to weave their way round us, but one pulled in front and a gentleman got out. He said he had a rope and would tow us to a garage. He then fastened the rope between our cars. Without thinking, in gratitude I said 'Oh, you are an angel'. My husband put the key in the ignition and our car roared into life. The man smilingly removed the now unnecessary rope and... disappeared. Honestly, we did not see him go.

Many people would argue that such encounters are merely people stopping and genuinely being helpful – a relatively rare occurrence, sadly, today. However, the authors of the accounts are all adamant that there was something extra special about their 'Good Samaritan'. Of course, we all get help from time to time with heavy shopping bags, but how many of us can recall the occasions with such vividness many years on? It is that which makes these experiences stand out.

Thought-provoking experiences

Some experiences seemingly occur to prompt a different way of thinking, or to help change a recipient's view on life. Such an event happened to Canon R. St L. Broadberry, while he was a student at Trinity College, Dublin, in 1952:

Before lunch I was enjoying an arrogant harangue against the Roman Catholic Church's doctrine with a fellow student... in the Theological Society at the top of the Graduates Memorial Building.

As we prattled on, the door opened and in came a college painter, dressed in the usual white overalls.

After a brief pause he questioned what we were saying and flicked over pages of a Bible and demolished what we were saying against the Doctrine of Original Sin by pointing to several verses of Scripture.

He then left and closed the door behind him. We were somewhat taken aback and looked at each other. We then looked to out to see where he had gone, but there was no sign of him on the staircase, or outside, and no workmen were working nearby. And if I remember rightly, we could not find him in the Philosophical or Historical Society Rooms on the other floors.

I was sure, and still am, that that day we were visited by an angel who cured us of our bigoted views at a stroke!

A similar incident experienced by Rev. D Footitt certainly helped him to take at long, hard look at his life. Being a devout atheist, gambler and slight alcoholic he always stayed at home when his wife went to church. One night, he heard a voice in the night; a week later he met a tramp while browsing in a bookshop. He took him for a drink and was told by the stranger all about his own life, helping him to reassess things. The tramp disappeared, and it turned out that other people in the pub had not seen him, presuming that Mr Footitt had been talking to himself. As a result of this extraordinary meeting, Mr Footitt went on to become a Christian Pentecostal minister.

A stranger also helped Pastor David Butcher reassess his own life one day when he received a knock on the door of his study. A stranger stood there and asked if he could come in and talk:

He seemed perfectly normal, perhaps a bit 'down'

emotionally. I had never seen him before and I have no idea of his name. He just said that he had a problem and needed advice. He began to pour out his heart to me, a total stranger.

Perhaps that might not seem too strange to you, or even to me. I began to answer him as honestly as I could both from common sense and from the Scriptures, as you might expect [of] a minister counselling someone. Suddenly, I almost stopped in my tracks. I had been wrestling with certain personal problems myself. They were so personal I felt that I could not go to anyone, that it was something which I had to battle through on my own. But there I was, dealing with an absolutely identical situation. I was giving him all the answers that I needed and was too blind to see for myself. He left and [...] walked down the road. I never ever heard from him or saw him again, which because of the intensity of his problem was quite strange. I wondered then and have often wondered since, did God send an angel to make me wake up to my own problems, to answer my own questions?'

Help getting home

The following accounts all describe incidents that took place when the people involved were experiencing some difficulty with their journeys:

We were on holiday in Tenerife in 1981. I was rushed to hospital with salmonella, followed by my son, Edward, [who was] ten months old. Because we were desperate to get home, we left the hospital after two weeks and sat waiting at the airport for a flight home.

It was the height of the holiday season. There we no flights. We prayed.

All of a sudden a lady dressed in bright blue appeared with blonde hair tied up on top. She smiled at me and said 'You're in trouble aren't you?' and handed me four tickets for the family. My husband George was amazed. We looked up to thank her, but she had disappeared. We believed she was an angel. We had heard of Billy Graham's book on angels, and we have told the events to many people over the years. Some offered explanations, others believed it. When we got on the plane we were sitting adjacent to George's mother and brother who had flown over to help us. God is good and sent an angel to rescue us from a difficult situation.

In 1956, Jennifer Jenkins was a student nurse at Charing Cross Hospital. At the time of the incident she describes, she was working at the outlying Hospital of Mount Vernon, Northwood in Middlesex, doing her TB training:

One evening, I and a fellow student nurse had been up to town for an evening of dancing and fun. We were due to catch the last train back but having been promised a lift and been let down, we were distraught and didn't know what to do, as we had only our train fares in cash and not enough for a taxi to Northwood. Apart from that, we were worried sick in case we should be caught coming in late by 'Nelly Kelly', the terrifying night sister, who patrolled the car park, looking for nurses who were out without a late pass! Those were the days when 'seniority' meant rules that must be obeyed!

We were standing on the pavement in Park Lane, on

a triangle of road near to the Dorchester Hotel. This part of the road had no buildings with doorways or alleyways, just railings around gardens and grass areas. We had hailed a taxi cab and were discussing with the driver just how far he could take us for the money we had between us. We were despairing and wondering how we'd walk the rest of the way back... Just at our most anxious moment, a gentleman in full evening dress appeared next to us inquiring what the problem seemed to be. We explained our plight and, without hesitation, he produced a note to cover the amount needed for our fare to the far-away hospital. The taxi driver looked at the money to check it was enough and we too stared at the note in disbelief. And as we turned to thank him, he was gone! We all looked in every direction, up and down the road but none of us could explain where he possibly could have disappeared to.

He was dressed in full evening dress, even with a white silk scarf, a sort of Fred Astaire figure. As we climbed into the welcome warmth of the cab, the driver exclaimed in disbelief that he surely must have been our guardian angel sent to look after us!

Given direction

Getting lost is a common worry – especially if en route to an important engagement. Jean Freeman, the woman who received unexpected help in the shape of a lady and her young baby when they climbed into her train carriage, had another experience that to her suggested divine intervention. This second incident happened many years after the first, but is connected to it:

I drove to a cousin's wedding and got lost missing the

turning to the church from the main road to Gatwick.
I had to keep going for a while and then I came to a
roundabout which had a garage on it. I went into the
forecourt in order to ask someone if they could help
me, but before I got out of the car, the same lady that
I had seen on Preston Road Station crossed the busy
road and came up to me. She was carrying a shopping
basket and asked if she could help me and when I said
where I wanted to go, she said she was shopping in
that area and would direct me. She got in the car and
directed me to the church. I sat there wondering
whether or not I should ask her who she was, but
somehow I felt dumbstruck. She got out at the church
and I managed to thank her, still looking at her in
amazement. She didn't have a halo, but on both
occasions wore an extraordinary tweed coat. When I
told my cousin of my experience he said 'But there are
no shops near the church!'

Dorothy Nicholls and her husband also received help with
directions from an unexpected source:

My husband felt called into the Baptist ministry. We
visited three of the Baptist Theological Training
Colleges: the one in London, the one in Bristol and
also Regent's Park College in Oxford.

After arriving and parking in the town of Oxford,
we were getting our bearings on foot to find the
college for an interview session. Suddenly 'out of the
blue', while we were silently pursuing our route, but
still not sure of the exact road, a man spoke to us.

He was, if I remember an older man of about sixty
years perhaps, dressed in an overcoat or mac, and

sitting on a roadside bench. What he said to us has amazed us to this day, as we were sure we were not talking aloud or specifically about our destination, at that particular moment. The words were something like, 'Are you looking for Regent's Park College?' We were. He then gave us directions and we continued our journey to the college.

An everyday experience perhaps, but to us, extra-ordinary. Paradoxically, my husband did not eventually study at Regent's Park, but at the Bristol Baptist College. However, we still recall the unusual, benign stranger that day.

A very similar thing happened to Janice West:

One evening, my husband and I, and a visitor from the Far East, had an experience of what we believe was an angel. We were driving in the dark, down narrow country lanes, trying to find the visitor's new lodging; all we had to go on was an address with no instructions on how to find it. As far we could see there were no houses along the lanes and there were no streetlights.

Eventually we found a small cul-de-sac, we drove into it and prayed together for guidance. Immediately, a car pulled up behind us and a pleasant man of about thirty walked to our car and asked if he could help us in any way. We told him we were trying to find an address and gave him the name of the people in the house we were looking for. He said 'Follow me'. We did so and eventually his car stopped at a gap in the roadside hedge. This we discovered was the obscure entrance to the narrow drive of the house we were looking for. My husband Adrian got out of the car to thank the stranger but he drove off.

We realised later that he could not have been a passing stranger, because he turned off the main lane into the cul-de-sac. He drove in after we had stopped and were praying. He could not by normal means have known we were there, nor that we were lost and seeking help. We have always felt that the man was an angel sent to help us in our moment of distress.

BLIND VISIONS: VISIONARY ANGELIC EXPERIENCES IN THE BLIND

'This life's dim windows of the soul

Distorts the heavens from pole to pole

And leads you to believe a lie

When you see with, not thro', the eye.'

William Blake, 'The Everlasting Gospel' (circa 1818)

I SIFTED THROUGH hundreds of letters received in response to my appeal for reports of encounters with angels. In the process of painstakingly entering them onto my database, I realised that three of the letters were particularly intriguing since the respondents were actually registered blind – one had been blind since birth – and related their experience, and the appearance of the angel, in the same way as a sighted person.

Barely anything has been written on the blind and visions in this type of context and I found it hard to know where to begin. Many books on the market outline near-death experiences, a few of which may contain a paragraph or so on a blind person who has had an experience. In fact, while writing a university paper[1] on my findings, I came across a study conducted by Dr. Kenneth Ring in which he tried to assess whether blind individuals have ever claimed to have 'seen' during near-death experiences (NDEs).[2] It was not particularly surprising to find that no research has been carried out using religious experience, let alone visionary (or indeed sensory) angelic experiences as the core.

> *'... like you see people, I see angels – pretty good deal I reckon!'*[3]
> *Stephanie Sergeant*

Of the three experiences that I received from blind people, one was from Stephanie Sergeant, who is a Christian and has been registered blind since birth due to micro thalmos bilateral congenital cataracts; she has her own guide dog. The second was from Ruth Albert, an extremely well-learned and intelligent Jewish-Buddhist lady who has had low vision since the age of about five, due to hereditary myopia. She was actually registered blind at the time of her experience, which took place when she was 54 years old, though since having a cataract removal operation back in April 1999, her sight — which incidentally was -21 (-7 is average sight) — has improved. Her left eye is still completely blind, but she now has low vision in her right eye thanks to her operation, which has improved her sight in this eye to +3. The third blind person who wrote to me was called Michael. His sight has progressively got worse, due to hereditary retinitis pigmentosa, since the age of about two. Michael is now in his early thirties, is severally visually impaired and can only make out light and dark; he has his own guide dog.

Stephanie told me that she has seen angels intermittently during the past 20 years or so, but her first angelic experience occurred when she was 24, alone and lost in London. Needing help to cross a busy road back in 1978 she was aided by a man, who was extremely patronising. During the crossing, Stephanie mentioned in conversation that she was a Christian. At this, the man scoffed and walked off, leaving her in the middle of the road surrounded by traffic either side! Immediately she 'saw' two angels either side of her, which guided her in safety to the other side. She relates the incident to me today in a very matter-of-fact manner. The experience did not perplex her in any way, so it seems — as she explained her beliefs to me, angels are the entities recorded in the Bible — just as Elijah saw angels the eyes of his servants were opened, as hers were. After the experience, Stephanie reveals that she spoke to God about it and through this communication her questions were answered.

Her most vivid experience happened in 1997, when Stephanie had just heard that her devoutly Christian father had died. She was travelling on a train from Birmingham to London Euston. Suddenly, '… through my tears… I could see the angels rejoicing that he had reached heaven.'[4] There were many angels in the carriage, glowing with light and very agile. They were singing beautifully and in harmony and the joy on their faces as they smiled cheered her up. As she wrote in her original letter, 'I'm blind, by the way, so I have never seen joy and smiles like that on any of my friends' faces, but now, having seen the angels, I can picture the expressions my friends describe. It makes life much more worth living.'

Ruth's first mystical experience occurred in April 1980. At the time she was very depressed (though not clinically) and after being taught how to meditate, decided to try it one night. Starting from 100 she began counting backwards, only to find that when she had finished, a warmth engrossed her, like a 'joyous throbbing pulse' settling in her heart. Over the next few days she began to feel nature differently, as if it were 'pulsating with the same love and joy' that she could feel —as if 'joy sprang up in [her] heart' and 'sunlight was streaming through the heavens in her mind's eye.'[5] She subsequently had many more mystical experiences. This experience, although not angelic in the sense that we have been exploring, was the turning point – it was as if from that point Ruth became open and receptive. She had always believed that God existed, but this experience transformed her life.

Back in 1995 Ruth was sitting in her armchair and looked up to 'see' an angel standing in the doorway – it was enormous, giving off powerful vibrations. She sat with her thesaurus on her lap and asked the question 'who is this?' – randomly opening the book her finger pointed to the words 'guardian angel'.

Since this occasion, Ruth has had numerous similar experiences, either through using angel cards or by means of a similar random reading, whereby she holds either the Bible or her thesaurus (given to her as a present for her 18th birthday) and asks a question, either to God, or sometimes her angel. Opening the book, she lets her finger run down the page until it stops at a select verse – 95 per cent of the time, she maintains, the verse corresponds to the question and gives her an accurate answer or prediction. However, she points out the dangers of this type of mysticism and states it should not be entered into lightly and only by those who know what they are doing. Back in April 1999 she was very nervous before her eye operation, and about to go for her pre-op she asked, 'Angel – will I be able to see?' and the verse she opened her bible to was 'and the angel answered and said unto thee, fear you not'. She also asked 'Will I be able to read' – the verse her finger pointed to was 1 Chronicles 28:19 – 'All this in writing at the Lord's direction, he made dear to me…'

Although not completely blind since birth, Michael has barely any recollection of what full sight is. A confirmed atheist, he is a very rational and logical man. His blindness does not prevent him from doing anything and he holds down a well-respected job at a firm of solicitors. Apart from his father and the nurses on shift at the time, no one else knows of his angelic experience – because it can't be explained rationally, Michael finds it hard to rationalise and, ultimately, to talk about.

Michael's mother had had a stroke; also being a diabetic made her condition all the more critical. Michael sat with his father at her bedside from the moment she had been rushed into hospital one Sunday morning. They remained there in the small intensive care ward until late Sunday evening. Suddenly, Michael was aware of an incredibly strong, sweet smell – something he can not compare to anything else and a smell he has never come across since. He asked his father what it could be; as they were in the ITU ward, there were no flowers or anything there that could have been the cause. (His father, incidentally, could not smell a thing.) Michael then 'saw' his mother's aged face 'bathed in a glorious light as if from heaven' – not at all how he remembered her. After a few minutes, Michael became increasingly agitated, with a sense of dread spreading across him. Moments later, his mother suddenly and silently passed away. 'Perhaps there is something there,' concedes Michael, though he is still not convinced. He questions why his father could not smell the scent, but believes it could have been a way of his mother saying a final farewell, or even preparing him, momentarily, for her departure. His father is a strong Christian and his son's experience has given him exceptional hope, encouraging him to believe that his wife is safe and well – he looks at the experience much more favourably, believing that this was his wife's goodbye to her only child.

This brings into question the spontaneity of such experiences. Although both Michael and his father knew the seriousness of his mother's condition, neither was prepared for her death to be (a) so peaceful and (b) so sudden. In other words, Michael was not aware anything was wrong – his mother was stable – and the experience occurred completely spontaneously and without warning. Rationally speaking, there was nothing there to trigger it.

The whole notion of blind people having visual angelic experiences is clearly a remarkable one. It might be explained by the fact that many registered blind people are in fact partially sighted. One common misconception regarding the blind is that they cannot see at all – Dr Kenneth Ring's article 'Near-Death and Out-of-Body Experiences in the Blind: A Study of Apparent Eyeless Vision', in the *Journal of Near Death Studies*, fuels this misunderstanding in its very title, by referring to 'eyeless vision'. Legally, a person is classified as blind when their visual resolution drops below a certain level. In other words, the majority of blind people can see the difference between light and dark and may be able to detect motion to a degree. The common belief that the blind are 'eyeless' therefore is not strictly speaking correct.

However, there are a number of other curious phenomena which, whilst not perhaps directly linked with angel experiences per se, put a very intriguing spin on my three respondents' experiences. These are near-death experiences in the blind and other phenomena such as blindsight and other medical diagnoses.

Visual near-death experiences and the blind

The whole question of whether blind individuals can actually see during out-of-body experiences (OBEs) has long intrigued researchers in the field of near-death studies.[6] Many physicians have published accounts of such events, including Larry Dossey, who opened his book *Recovering the Soul* (1989) with the dramatic case of a woman named Sarah, blind from birth, who had a detailed visual perception during surgery whilst her heart had stopped. However, this account, along with several others, turned out to be nothing more than mere fabrication – Dossey later confessed in a communication with Kenneth Ring that it was complete fiction, though he justified it on the grounds that such cases seem to be implied. Many books outline cases of the alleged visions experienced by people who have been congenitally blind from birth, only for the book's next edition to omit these cases on the grounds that the case has been proven false.

Admittedly, I found it hard to find a substantiated account of someone who claimed to 'see' what a sighted person would see during an NDE. However, below are two cases that I feel, although not angelic in content, are still of interest to this debate.

Brad Barrows had been blind since birth. When he was eight years old, and a student at the Boston Centre for Blind Children Brad contracted a severe case of pneumonia and developed severe breathing difficulties. His heart had actually stopped for four minutes, during which time he had to be resuscitated by CPR.[7]

Brad remembers that when he couldn't breathe any longer, he felt himself lifting up from the bed and floating through the room towards the ceiling. He saw his apparently lifeless body on the bed. He also saw his roommate get up from his bed to get help (the roommate later confirmed that he had done so). Brad then felt himself rapidly going upward through the ceilings of the building until he was above the roof – at which point he found that he could see clearly. He estimates that it was between 6:30 and 7:00 a.m. when this happened. He noticed the sky was cloudy and dark – there had been a snowstorm the day before and Brad could see snow everywhere except on the streets, which had been ploughed, though they were still slushy. He was able to provide a very detailed description of the way the snow looked – Brad could also see the snowbanks the ploughs had created. He saw a streetcar go by. Finally, he recognised a playground used by the children of his school and a particular hill he used to climb nearby.

When asked if he 'knew' or 'saw' these things, he replied 'I clearly visualised them. I could suddenly notice them and see them… I remember… being able to see quite clearly'. After this segment of the experience, which happened very fast, was over, he found himself in a tunnel and emerged from it to find himself in an immense field illuminated by a tremendous, all-encompassing light. Everything was perfect.

Brad could clearly see in this domain too, though he commented that he was puzzled by the sensation of sight. He found himself walking on a path surrounded by tall grass, and also reported seeing tall trees with enormous leaves. No shadows were visible, however.

While he was in this field, Brad became aware of beautiful music, a sound like nothing he had ever heard on earth. Walking towards the source of the music, he came to a hill, which he climbed, and eventually encountered a glittering stone structure so brilliant that he thought it might be burning hot. But it wasn't and he entered it. The music continued here as well and, to Brad, it seemed to be praising God. In this structure, Brad encountered a man he didn't recognise but from whom emanated an overwhelming love. The man, without a word, gently nudged Brad backwards, initiating a reversal of his experience, ending with him finding himself in bed gasping for air, attended by two nurses.

The second experience I want to share with you is that of Vicki Umipeg[8], who, like Brad has been blind since birth. Vicki was born very prematurely at 22 weeks and weighing just 3lbs; her weight subsequently dropped to 1lb 14oz. As was common with premature babies in the 1950s, she was placed in an airlock incubator through which oxygen was administered. However, Vicki was given too much oxygen and, along with about 50,000 other premature babies born in the USA at the same time, suffered such optic nerve damage as to leave her completely blind. As she made clear in an initial interview with researcher Greg Wilson, she has never had any visual experience whatever:

Interviewer: Could you see anything?
Vicki: Nothing, never. No light, no shadows, no nothing ever.
Interviewer: So the optic nerve was destroyed in both eyes?
Vicki: Yes, and so I've never been able to understand even the concept of light.

In 1973, Vicki was working as an occasional singer in a nightclub in Seattle. One night after finishing her set, Vicki found herself unable to find a taxi to drive her home. Circumstances forced her to take the only other option: a ride in a van with a couple of inebriated patrons. Not surprisingly, a serious accident ensued, during which Vicki was thrown out of the van. Her injuries were extensive and life threatening, and included a skull fracture and concussion, and damage to her neck, back and one leg. In fact, it took her a full year before she could stand upright without the risk of fainting.

Vicki clearly remembers the frightening prelude to the crash itself, but only has a hazy recollection of finding herself out of her body and seeing the crumpled vehicle and her body. She has no memory of the trip to hospital, but while in the emergency room, found herself up on the ceiling, watching doctors working on her body. She overheard their conversation and concerns that she may become deaf due to damage to her eardrums. Almost immediately she found herself going up through the ceilings of the hospital until she was above the roof of the building, during which time she had a panoramic view of her surroundings. At this time she also heard harmonious music, akin to wind chimes.

With scarcely a noticeable transition, she then discovered she had been sucked headfirst into a tube. The enclosure was dark, yet she was aware that she was moving toward light until she was eventually 'rolled out' of the tube to find herself lying on grass, surrounded by trees and flowers and a vast number of people. Vicki then saw five people whom she knew, including two old school friends, who had been slightly retarded and who had died aged six and eleven; however, here they were made of light – beautiful, healthy and seemingly 'in their prime'. She also saw two of her childhood carers and her grandmother. She had a sense of 'knowing everything... like everything made sense' and was flooded with information of a religious, scientific and mathematical nature. As these revelations were unfolding, Vicki noticed a figure next to her whose radiance was far greater than that of the others. Immediately she recognised this being as Jesus. He showed Vicki her life from birth until the present. Then she was told she couldn't stay and had to return to have her children. With that she experienced a 'sickening thud' and found herself back inside her body, feeling heavy and full of pain.

Blindsight

There is a clear similarity between dreams and visions among the blind. However short-sighted people are, their dreams are never blurred and indistinct – they see as clearly as they would when wearing their glasses or contact lenses.[9] It seems the same is true with the above case studies – both partially sighted and visually impaired respondents had no trouble in recognising or describing in vivid detail what they saw – the experience was viewed with complete clarity.

Near-death experiences are regarded by many as not being viewed through the 'real eyes', but brought about by seeing images that have previously been seen and stored in the brain. All this is very well – when people are dreaming or experience a NDE, either through trauma or from illness, then the body is in a different state to that of an alert person who is healthy and awake. Could the type of vision produced during a NDE, or OBE be explained through an altered state in consciousness? Surely an angelic experience, or certainly the ones I have outlined above, are experienced in a completely different way?

Dreams are viewed in many cultures as being seen through a different eye – a third eye. This concept relates to another important phenomenon relevant here – that of 'blindsight' – which could well be one factor in cases such as those outlined above.

A recent article in *New Scientist*[10] explores the area of blindsight and its relation to consciousness, highlighting the fact that '[many researchers], from neuroscientists armed with brain scanners to philosophers and experts in artificial intelligence... treat blindsight with great respect these days...'

As an eight-year-old, a man referred to by *New Scientist* as Graham ran into the path of a moving car, which struck him in the back of the head.[11] Immediately in the wake of the accident, doctors feared for Graham's life and presumed at the very least that he would suffer significant brain damage. However, miraculously, the damage was limited to the left-hand part of a section of brain tissue situated towards the back of the head, known as V1. This area acts as one of the main receptors of information from the retina. Ironically perhaps, due to the injuries he suffered from his accident, Graham has subsequently become much in demand by psychologists and neuroscientists, so much so that he currently spends only half of his working week carrying out his work as a psychiatric nurse. Indeed, during one year he participated in 29 separate experiments, each lasting approximately three days.

Technically speaking, Graham's accident has given him blindsight. He cannot see anything to the right of his focal point, either with his left or right eye. However, in scientific experiments he has demonstrated that he is capable of reaching out and grasping objects, finding spots of light on a screen and carrying out other tasks that, to the conventional way of thinking, would require full vision. Graham himself says that such achievements feel like the product of simple guesswork to him.

The reason that science has taken such an interest in him, however, is that he is apparently 'seeing' unconsciously. If a bright light is flashed quickly enough in front of him, he registers movement, though he usually characterises it as a dark shadow; lights or objects that are moved quickly enough seem to register with him as 'pure movement', with no shape, volume or colour. Graham's condition suggests that consciously seeing an object is not the only way of perceiving it. And he is not alone in being so gifted. Early research in this field revolved around a monkey named Helen that, like Graham, lacked part of her V1 brain tissue – usually considered vital for effective vision – and yet demonstrated herself capable of distinguishing objects and reaching for food.

Graham's unusual condition remained a secret, even to him, until researchers at London's Imperial College, led by the late Keith Ruddock, began testing him in the late 1970s. Rigorous experiments proved that Graham wasn't using his good field of vision to see objects. Indeed, rather than allowing blindsight subjects to tell them what they see, researchers simply study changes in the pupils of their eyes in order to gauge their perceptive abilities; the pupils contract slightly when stimulated visually.

There is still some scientific debate as to the significance of blindsight. Some researchers believe it is simply a diluted form of normal vision and argue that although visual signals leave the retina and move along the usual pathways to the brain, they are too weak to result in conventional vision. According to this theory, rather than having lost the ability to produce visual consciousness, the brains of blindsight sufferers are simply incapable of processing basic visual information.

Larry Weiskrantz, an Oxford psychologist who has made a major contribution towards raising scientific awareness of blindsight over the past quarter century, does not hold with the idea that blindsight is simply a weakened form of normal sight. Graham has vision in one field and blindness in the other; however, he has proved himself capable of considerable levels of perception in both fields and in some experiments, actually achieved better results in his blind field than in his field of normal vision. If he simply had degraded vision, scientists could conclude that he lacked sight – there would be no need to argue that his brain lacked visual consciousness; visual consciousness and visual perception would then have to be regarded as being the same thing, produced by the same mechanisms in the brain. Weiskrantz disagrees, arguing that Graham and his fellow blindsight sufferers are capable of detecting visual stimuli such as wavelengths, but not able to translate that into visual consciousness – for example, the 'redness' of the colour red, what makes it the colour that it is. According to this theory, something else is required, apart from the ability to perceive objects visually, in order for the brain to make that cognitive step.

Weiskrantz believes that brain scans may offer a clue as to that missing element in the visual process. MRI (magnetic resonance imaging) brain scanners analyse the functions of the brain rather than its structure. By putting a blindsight sufferer in an MRI brain scanner and asking them to perform a visual task in both their blind and normal vision fields and mapping the results of one on top of the other, it may be possible to discover whether there is a difference in the way the brain processes vision with awareness (i.e. simple visual perception) and vision without awareness. Experiments currently taking place in a number of laboratories seem to suggest that there is indeed a difference.

Analysis of Graham's brain in such test conditions seems to indicate that there is a difference in the quantity of brain activity registered in conscious seeing and unconscious seeing. When he becomes aware of something in his blindfield, the front of Graham's cortex registers a higher degree of activity than that of the lower regions of the brain. There is also activity in a structure situated in the middle of the brain, called the superior colliculus. As Graham's primary receptor for receiving right-field visual stimuli – the V1 brain tissue – is damaged, visual information must travel along alternative routes that bypass this area. And these routes pass through the superior colliculus. Such secondary information routes, Weiskrantz believes, operate in all of us, although not to the degree that they do in sufferers of cortex blindness. 'It would be a waste of effort for the brain to spend time making events conscious that don't really require it,' he explains. 'There are lots of times in life [when] we carry out visual discriminations without any awareness at all. It's when we're going on automatic pilot.' Considering that Graham's blindfield is triggered by rapidly moving objects and sudden flashes, it is possible that blindsight is part of the body's early warning defence system.

Blindsight has very marked limitations, however, as an aid to perception. Anthony Marcel, who works at the Medical Research Council's Cognition and Brain Sciences Unit in Cambridge, notes that Graham is not able to use blindsight to help him reach a glass of water, even if he is exceptionally thirsty, unless someone tells him that the glass is there in the first place. Neither does his blindsight allow Graham to retain images of objects: 'I can't replicate the sensation of an event in my imagination,' he explains. 'I know that little about it. I can't actually go home and think that's what it looked like to me.'

Interestingly, blindsight appears to be a condition that allows improved degrees of perception over time. Graham's perceptive skills have improved over the last few years; he requires lower levels of brightness and less rapid movements to sense objects than he did previously. However, despite the fact that Graham can distinguish and discriminate between shapes, movements and wavelengths in his blind field, no scientist has so far been able to explain to him why he can't see objects themselves. Clearly, science still has much to discover about the phenomenon of blindsight, and the nature of consciousness.

Charles Bonnet Syndrome

'Charles Bonnet Syndrome is diagnosed when a visually impaired person without any mental disorder develops visual hallucination.'[12]

In 1760, Charles Bonnet described the occurrence of vivid visual hallucinations (VH) in his psychologically normal, but visually impaired, grandfather. He described them as 'amusing and magical visions co-existing with reason'. In 1982, Charles Bonnet Syndrome was defined by the scientist J. Damas-Mora as a persistent recurrent visual hallucinatory phenomena of a pleasant or neutral nature, with a clear state of consciousness, compelling but seen by the patient as unreal. It is generally associated with diseases of the eye, and tends to be remarkably crisp, detailed and, at times, Lilliputian. Since Charles Bonnet's time, many reports of isolated episodes of VH have been reported. During the 19th century, Bonnet's description became the paradigm for the existence of VH in the sane. Clinicians are more likely to encounter cases of what has been termed Charles Bonnet Syndrome Plus, in which VH are associated with other psychopathology or neurological disorders.

A case presentation from a website, Grand Rounds at Froedtert Hospital[13], outlines risk factors that could increase the chance of a blind person encountering VH. These factors include living alone or social isolation. However, what is important to this study is the mention in the presentation of bereavement being 'a risk factor for VH in the elderly'. In a study of widowed spouses, hallucinations of the deceased spouse occurred in 69% of the widows; 85.7% of these experiences were reported as good. Altogether, 76% of the 46 widows reported some sort of hallucinatory experience. Fifty-four per cent stated they had never discussed the experiences with anyone prior to the interview.

Such data indeed ties in with the accounts that I have received. Two of the respondents had visions after the death of a loved one – Michael's experience occurred in the minutes leading up to his mother's death and during her passing, and Stephanie's experience was a short time after hearing the news of her father's illness. Neither had spoken about the experience before writing a letter to me, for fear of being ridiculed or not believed.

Depression is something else that seems to be closely connected to patients with symptoms associated with Charles Bonnet Syndrome, and also something Ruth speaks of suffering at the time. The case presentation notes that, 'Assessment and treatment of visual problems as well as diagnosis and treatment of psychiatric problems including depression are important. Assessment of a loss history to establish bereavement issues may provide opportunities to do grief work. Grief work has been shown to stop VH and eliminate the potential side-effects from controversial medication trials. Management of the environment such as moving a patient to a less isolated place and increasing stimulation has been shown to be helpful.'[14] Analysing the respondents to this study more closely, it appears that Stephanie was certainly grieving and her experience was of a similar type.

Judging by the material I have read through, however, CBS does seem to be a clinical condition associated purely 'with the elderly.'[15] This would suggest that the condition might not relate very closely to the experiences of my two aforementioned respondents – Stephanie was only 43 years old at the time of her experience and Michael was 27.

Analysing the total number of narrative accounts received, out of the 350 letters, 58% of them occurred during a time of terminal illness or an impending life-threatening situation for either the respondent or a close relation. This fact ties in with the findings outlines in chapter nine, 'Angels of Death'. However, the whole area of grief study is vast and goes far beyond the space that I could devote to it in this book.[16]

Anton's Syndrome

Anton's Syndrome, or cortial blindness, consists of blindness, denial of blindness and at times confabulation (in which an individual devises imaginary experiences after the loss of memory). Despite the fact that the patient is completely blind, they persistently deny that they are unable to see, a trait that is sometimes accompanied by visual hallucinations.[17]

I do not think that any of the recipients to this study suffer from this condition, however; for one thing, none of them had even heard of the condition before I mentioned it to them, let alone been diagnosed as sufferers. Besides, in the cases of both Stephanie and Michael, the vision was spontaneous, a fact that, if I understand it correctly, would distinguish it from this syndrome.

Conclusions

Although the idea of a blind angel vision is widely open to scepticism, there is, as I hope I have explained, a large body of research to suggest that there are blind people who do believe that they've had 'visions' of angels; hopefully my findings during my research at the University of Birmingham will add significantly to this set of data. I think, bearing the above in mind, the conception of an 'eyeless vision' does not seem so unfeasible, or even miraculous, as perhaps it appeared at first.

From the results, it is quite apparent that these people have undergone some sort of experience. It is interesting to note the varied nature of blindness amongst the recipients – be it blindness caused from an eye disorder, disease, or from birth. Even more interesting is the fact that each of the experiences were similar – both to each other's as well as to those experiences of individuals who had perfect sight.

Ruth reported seeing a traditional angel figure, although her religious beliefs run more towards a Buddhist spirituality than to Christianity. Stephanie, who has been blind since birth, also saw a traditional angel; such a description could have been orally passed on to her, but her account of the experience and the language and vocabulary used to verbalise it makes me think that she did actually experience such a sight – be it internal or external. I am, however, surprised that I did not receive more accounts of physical forces, touches or scents among blind and partially sighted respondents such as Michael.

Complex visual 'hallucinations' may affect some normal individuals as they drift off to sleep – the very fact that a high percentage of my respondents had their experience in the bedroom, although adamant that they were awake at the time, is striking. Such hallucinations bring to mind notions of sleep paralysis, old hag tales and lucid dreaming. Hallucinations are also evident in pathological states, often in association with a sleep disturbance.[18] It seems that the content of these hallucinations is striking and relatively stereotyped, often resulting in the person seeing animal and human figures that are set off from a striking, sometimes bizarre, setting. Many conditions could be the possible cause of such an experience – migraine (although this condition usually results in symmetrical patterns, crescent shapes and the like), Parkinson's Disease, schizophrenia, epilepsy, hallucinogen-induced states, meditative states and so on. However, none of these are necessarily the cause of the experiences reported by any of the respondents to this study, as it seems unlikely that they have any undiagnosed medical conditions.

I believe that visual hallucinations in the blind are common. By considering only those visions that are of a religious nature, however, or even further, by stipulating that the experience must be angelic, it is possible to start to distinguish these visual experiences from those caused by medical conditions.

Because I am neither medically nor philosophically trained, I can not make assumptions nor prognoses regarding the medical conditions above. However, such conditions can not be avoided in a study such as this – whether they are likely to be contributory factors to the experience or not.

Conclusions drawn from the whole area of blind people and visions as a whole, if this was proven so, would be vast – the fact that blind people are claiming to 'see' angels would mean taking into account issues and arguments of whether experiences are culturally determined as well as the language used to describe such encounters would all be thrown into complete disarray.

ANGEL
VOICES

'It was a male voice, very clear and very distinct.
It wasn't a voice I recognised, but somehow I knew it
was a good voice. My mother said something that
I hadn't thought of. She said "Maybe it was your
guardian angel."'

ONE MORNING Sue Moss was lying in bed with her baby daughter after her husband had left early to get to work. Exhausted after a bad night's sleep, she slept in to be woken by a voice reiterating the words 'Your baby's in the road'. Unable to ignore the voice, Sue rolled over and realised her daughter wasn't in bed beside her. She rushed out of the bedroom to find that in his haste, her husband hadn't caught the latch on the front door when he'd left that morning. Her daughter had crawled from the bed to the front door and was now shuffling down the garden path towards the busy main road.

Throughout recorded history, angels have appeared and otherwise communicated with humans – indeed, the word 'angel' is originally derived from the ancient Greek 'angelos', which translates as 'messenger'. In antiquity, this is precisely what an angel was thought to be – a mouthpiece for God's will.

The idea, therefore, of angels bringing messages or warnings is not a new one. The angels' primary function within all scriptures is to be divine emissaries, with references made to them far back in Greek mythology and Hindu scripts. It was the Persian angel Vohu Manah who revealed God's message to the prophet Zoroaster some 2,500 years ago, while the Archangel Gabriel dictated the Koran to Mohammed a thousand years later. It was also Gabriel that told Mary she was to give birth to Jesus, while it was an angel that appeared to the shepherds to tell them the good news of Jesus's birth. Of course, angels are prevalent throughout the Hebrew and Christian Bible, bringing comfort and acting as intermediaries between man and God, as well as acting as guardians to people on earth.

The following accounts are from people who have not 'seen' an angel, but who believe they have heard one. The angels in these cases manifest themselves in the form of a voice, perhaps giving a warning message, words that have occasionally saved a life, uttering words of reassurance or at other times emitting beautiful music.

A life-saving warning

In 1970, Judith White was looking after her parents' house while they were away – she was in charge of the dog and the solid-fuel central-heating system, which provided her with hot water each day as long as she banked it up each night with solid fuel. 'I was told that the boiler had a propensity to go out, which would leave me with no hot water,' she explains, 'so I was to make sure to place enough coal on each evening...'

The first few days were fine, and I seemed to be coping well with everything, and then I awoke one morning to no hot water. The fire in the boiler had gone out. This was such a nuisance as I had to relight it again, and this wasn't an easy job to do. Then, to my annoyance, the following morning I discovered the same thing had happened again, and no hot water! I decided that perhaps I wasn't putting enough coal on the fire at night, and so that evening put a little extra on, hoping that this time the fire in the boiler would stay in.

In those days, as [soon as] my head hit the pillow I was asleep, and never stirred until my alarm went off at 7 a.m., and sometimes even that didn't wake me. However, this night I was awoken at 3 a.m. in the morning. I wasn't dreaming as there were no images in my head, but I was aware of someone standing next to my bed, bending over me and saying continuously in my ear, 'Judith wake up. The boiler's overheating.'

I sat bolt upright in bed, in the pitch black, but could see no one, even when I eventually put my light on. The voice was so insistent, that I decided to go and investigate the boiler, which was situated in the kitchen, the opposite end of the bungalow to my bedroom. When I entered the kitchen... the dog wasn't in her basket, which was placed next to the boiler, but sat in the middle of the floor looking rather perplexed. I looked at the temperature gauge on the boiler and it was on zero. 'Oh no, it's gone out again!' I said to myself, 'so much for the boiler overheating'. So I decided to light it again and when I opened the door, I was amazed to see rather fierce flames. I just couldn't understand what was going on, until I took a second look at the temperature gauge. It wasn't on zero at all, but the needle had gone all the way round. The boiler was indeed overheating. I didn't know what on earth to do. How do I put the fire out? Do I throw cold water over it?

When the noise started, I knew I had to get out. The pipes started to really bang, and I was aware that this was a dangerous situation. So I picked up the dog, and in dressing gown and nightie, went next door and eventually woke up our neighbour, Dave. Dave soon had the situation under control, by turning on all the hot taps, and releasing all the hot cinders. By 4 a.m. everything was back to normal, and he advised me to use the immersion heater in future, and forget about the boiler.

When my parents returned, Dave came to see them. He told them how serious the situation with the boiler had been. He said it was very fortunate that I awoke when I did, as the boiler was near to exploding. My mother asked me how I managed to wake, as she knew how heavily I normally slept. I told her about the voice. It was a male voice, very clear and very distinct. It wasn't a voice I recognised, but somehow I knew it was a good voice. My mother said something that I hadn't thought of. She said 'Maybe it was your guardian angel.'

Within weeks my parents had had the solid-fuel heating system removed, and replaced with an oil-fired central-heating [system], and it is there to this very day. I am a Christian, and I do believe in angels, although I have only had that one encounter, and my life was saved. I believe it was saved for a purpose, as I am now heavily involved in youth work in my church, and that is what I was always meant to do, I am absolutely sure of it.'

Another voice saved John Parkes. One weekend he was travelling home from the marines on his motorbike along roads near his grandparents that he knew really well. 'It was a perfect clear day and the roads were in good condition. I approached a bad left-hand bend bordered by a high hawthorn bush. On the apex, I slammed into the front of a low-loading lorry...'

The driver had cut the corner and [had] not seen my bike over the hedge. The bike was taken under the lorry and I went through the front windscreen. I passed through the cab of the truck and out through a glass panel in the rear. I was later to find out the driver had been using the van without permission from work to move house. I had passed between him and his wife and over his seven-year-old daughter's head.

After passing through the second pane of glass, I hit the wooden tailboard on the rear and was flipped into a ditch on the opposite corner of the road. This was related to me by accident investigators much later.

It is hard to say where my feeling began in all this; I have no recollection of pain until much later at A&E. I suffered fractures of both arms, radius and ulna, and dislocation of both elbows and knees; more importantly I broke five ribs, one of which punctured my right lung.

My clearest memory of the whole event was travelling upwards from the crash scene at high speed but with no feeling of inertia, or for that matter fear. When I stopped I could see the lorry stopped on the bend and me lying in a ditch, almost a dot. A man was clambering down the ditch towards me and a woman was standing behind him on the road. I have tried many times since to remember what the woman looked like or what she wore but when I think of her my mind goes blank – [it's] not just that I can't remember, [it just goes] completely blank. Sometimes if I cannot sleep I try to remember her and drop off.

I had this sense of warmth behind me but did not feel the need to look; it was warmth given by the brightest of lights. Then a single voice, female, with no sense of panic, telling me to roll over, repeatedly to roll over. I was suddenly in the ditch inside my body with the man. He was removing my helmet – later he said he could see blood. Although I could no longer hear the voice in the true sense of the word, it repeated in my mind, and I could clearly see the woman behind the man. I began to roll onto my side.

Difficult with such badly broken arms. The man fought to roll me back and remove my helmet, but somehow I won the battle of will.

I was later to find out that had I stayed on my back or rolled the other way I would probably have drowned, blood from the bad lung going into the good one. It took seven minutes for the ambulance to arrive. Very quick, but enough time to die. Later, giving statements, I mentioned the woman as a possible witness; however, the only female at the crash site was the driver's wife who never left the cab.

A word at the right time

Three months after a relationship split, Paul Dunwell experienced three 'visitations'...

All at night – on successive nights – but [none of them had] the texture of dream. In each, a figure, male I think, in white, stood to my left. On each occasion he said, simply, 'You have a child though no one has told you.' But since 'he' was featureless, I cannot be sure whether he spoke or projected these words. Yet I 'heard' them. Unlike most dreams these were vivid, so vivid that they rattled me and I discussed them with friends who put them down to an overactive imagination. However, after the third occasion, I rang my ex, who denied being pregnant. Ultimately, as it happened, she called me when our daughter... was three weeks old. She told me she'd be on the point of having her adopted at birth when the recollection of my dreams convinced her otherwise. And, she claimed, I'd known she was pregnant before she had herself. Was this an angel? I don't know, but [I've] never had a remotely similar experience before or since. After I'd listened, the 'dreams' stopped.

On two occasions, Frank Might has heard a voice whispering in his ear – 'one was going with a friend to Paris, and in the phone box making arrangements, I felt as thought someone had whispered in my ear "Do not go" and I did not. When unfortunately my own mother took her life, something said to me "go to communion for her", which I did.'

Sam Paynton was driving her car, 'admittedly a little fast', when she heard a voice warning her 'too fast' and physically felt her foot lift off gas pedal.

W. Raymond Shaw wrote, telling me 'At the age of about nine I was aware of being very ill and I think I was probably threatening meningitis...'

> I was lying very still in a darkened bedroom at home and my father came to my bedside and in a way of praying said something like 'Don't die, son'. I immediately replied 'I'm not going to die because the lady has told me.'
>
> The 'lady' was a figure that had come and stood at the foot of the bed, but on reflection it could have been a youth. The age was about sixteen; long, sallow, unsmiling serious face; long, flaxen hair. The dress was not white but of heavy blue or greenish brocade buttoned at the neck and there was just a suggestion of wing tips.

An angelic choir
Rod Treseder, a Sufi and practising Christian, settled down to sleep one night, but soon he became 'acutely aware of being in an inky blackness where I alone existed...'

Suddenly, from the void, I heard the most sublime music and singing – quite ineffable... I made an enormous effort to identify the words separately and eventually I succeeded! To my amazement they were singing only five words but repeated endlessly. The five words express the true relationship between God and man and the purpose of human existence in relationship to God. I only learned in later years that these words lie at the heart of Sufism, particularly as expounded by the great Sufi teacher Ibn Arabi. I believe these words were a divine revelation mediated by an angelic choir.

Mary Spain has also been 'privileged to hear the angels sing'[7] and Jane Monforte 'heard a Christmas carol 'Silent Night – Holy Night'' in her right ear in the middle of the night. 'I got up thinking it was the telly or [the] neighbours' telly [...] I even put my finger in my ear when I got back in bed. It was so beautiful when I finally settled down, accepting what I could hear. This was June last year, not Christmas time.'

Jackie Greedy recalled that when she was going through her 'dark night of the soul time' she 'had angels appear to her at a Black Madonna Shrine in Racamedeur, France. Then for a couple of years, I finally realised they made my phone "ding" in the early morning and at bedtime when I was having the worst times. I know we have angel visitors...'

During the Second World War, Joyce Trott was serving in the army by Widford and Housdon in Hertfordshire 'to develop an aerodrome in this area a church had to be demolished...'

As you know, there is a normal rule that a church is sacred and should not be tampered with. Anyway, one

night I was cycling back with a colleague to our billet
[...] as we passed by the area of the old church, we
saw an angel standing all in white with an organ
playing in the background. I might tell you, we could
not cycle away fast enough! We had already been told
about this experience by some forces men and women
who were stationed nearby at Hunson Aerodrome.

Angelic reassurance

A year or so ago Harry Lovelock was going through 'a
dreadfully traumatic time, I really was at my wits' end...'

> I lay in bed as near despair as I ever want to be.
> Suddenly interrupting my thoughts came a small
> voice, a tiny, but crystal clear voice that made itself
> heard as a triangle might amidst the crescendo of a
> hundred-piece orchestra. It simply said 'Keep going'. I
> relaxed and slept. The next day I was able to move
> forward.

Another correspondent wrote of a similar experience that
occurred 'when I was lying in bed awake one morning. I was
experiencing inner distress through a feeling of isolation when
I distinctly "heard" an extremely beautiful, unearthly voice
saying 'I love you, which was most comforting.'

Eileen Brebner wrote 'before my son was born thirty-seven
years ago, a man in a business suit, white shirt and tie came
into my bedroom. He said he had come to reassure me that all
would be well, as he was my guardian angel and would be
looking after me. I felt no fear, only a great sense of calm. In
spite of many difficulties with the birth, all was well and I was
able to give birth to my daughter three years later also.'

As a child, Ann Holmes was 'at home, lying in bed in the

daytime. My mother had gone out to do some shopping and I had got some childish ailment (I do not remember what it was now). I felt nervous at being on my own in the house. I looked towards the open door of my bedroom and the whole entrance to the room was filled with a very bright light. Then a voice, which seemed to come from me, strangely, said the words, 'Do not worry, I am with you.' In my childish way, I thought that it was a fairy. I don't think that I had heard of angels at that time but, looking back now, I think it must have been one.'

Back in 1995, Felicity Jane Dyson was 'feeling very low and sorry for myself thinking that the Lord had not recognised any of my merits or virtues and had blessed many of my friends – seemingly much less worthy…'

> I was walking through a wood with my little dog – and as I say, really very gloomy. Suddenly I felt a presence by my side (I did not see anything) and I heard a voice speaking to me internally. It said 'But you have trust in God' – as if having faith in God is a blessing, though not a visible one which perhaps these other friends lacked. I felt great [consolation] and joy. I just can not describe the sense that I felt, it was so beautiful it was indescribable. I wondered later if I had imagined it all, but I do not think so, as there was nothing else to account for such an overwhelming sense of consolation.

When Tracy Anne O'Mara moved to England recently from Australia she 'experienced a lot of anxiety and alienation. During this immensely emotional period I woke in the night to hear tinkling bells. As soon as I became fully conscious the bells ceased, I have also woken in the night to feel a presence behind me in bed holding me, but again, as soon as I became fully conscious the sensation ceased.' Another time she was woken in the night and saw 'a ball of white light hovering against the window. A loud voice said to me "This is available for you"... I knew it to be some kind of God force or my higher self talking to me.'

Michael had left home to rethink his religious views – after being brought up a Jehovah's Witness, he wanted to explore Anglicanism. His mother was most upset at his decision and couldn't sleep the night he left. In the early hours of the morning a white figure appeared to her at the foot of the bed and said 'Don't worry, Michael will be alright' and then vanished.

The following experience took place in the form of a voice which, to Winifred Wright, sounded like a 'golden trumpet'. Winifred's husband had died six months previously, leaving her to bring up their three small children alone. One night in bed, she heard a beautiful voice saying to her 'arise for this is not your rest'. She sat up and looked all around, but could see no one. With the babies to look after and work to do next day she failed to 'arise', thinking that to get up in the middle of the night and pray would be impractical. Now in her eighties, Winifred still felt she needed forgiveness for ignoring that command so many years ago, until recently she heard the voice again, telling her 'not now that you are ill, that was for when you were working'. After this second experience she is thankful.

To close this chapter, an incident that, while not featuring an angel as such, does feature an otherworldly voice. 'Our labrador Bodger, of fond renown hereabouts, died in 1982,' Doreen Lloyd wrote to me.

My husband went to sea so we had installed a burglar alarm system. At 2:30 a.m. one morning I awoke to hear my back door being tried. Before I could decide to press the panic button, ring the police, or lock myself in the lavatory and call for help, the great booming bark of our labrador, sometime deceased, barked out; the two cats on the bed looked up. We live at the end of the terrace, and have grass around the house, but after a short while I heard a car drive away. My husband also heard Bodger's bark on his return home from sea... so our Angelheart, which is what we called him, came to save me from a burglar.

HEAVEN
SCENT

'As I lay in the dark the most exquisite scent of
flowers filled the room – better than hyacinths, lilies
or orange blossom, but similar – it really was like
nothing I have ever smelt before or since...'

As DISCUSSED IN chapter one, smelling a beautiful fragrance and attributing its source to being angelic has been a common experience. This 'scent' crops up amid many experiences, especially visionary ones, examples of which are threaded throughout this book. Listed below, however, are experiences in which an otherworldly presence is detected purely by a scent, with no visual accompaniment. In this first section, a handful of experiences outline smelling a fragrance sometimes described as potpourri, roses or lavender.

Smelling a distinct scent is frequently connected with seeing ghosts or other paranormal sightings and occurrences. Such cases have been documented throughout the centuries, albeit not by scientifically 'reliable' sources. However, although it's a possibility, I do not think that the cases I have received share many common factors with well-documented experiences, such as that of St Teresa of Avila. When she died on October 4 1582, one nun said that 'Christ and an angelic host attended her passing and others said that she died in an ecstasy'. Soon after, an inexplicably sweet scent pervaded the convent – only a nun with sinus problems failed to detect it. 1 Hildegard of Bingen and Julian of Norwich also documented such experiences, along with other mystics.

As in the cases of auditory and visionary experiences, one needs to assess whether this is an internal or external experience. The medical terminology and psychiatric answers all revolve around olfactory hallucinations – in other words, that such experiences are brain induced. The symptom of smelling a particular scent may occur to epileptics and schizophrenics, though the scent in such cases tends to be an unpleasant, pungent, recurring odour rather than the beautiful one-off scent that many recipients have reported.

Some years ago, Peter Howell had an experience that he still cannot explain to his own satisfaction:

> I [was staying] with a friend near the Lizard. We were travelling in a car and approaching a road junction when I noticed something in the road. We stopped and I got out to remove the obstruction, which turned out to be a length of pipe, probably from the exhaust of another vehicle. I placed it on the grass verge where its owner could find it and we resumed our journey.
>
> The car was suddenly filled with the scent of lavender, which lasted for several minutes and then faded. The other occupants thought that this was the most natural thing in the world but I am still at a complete loss as to how to explain it.

The same scent was smelt by Muriel Duffy while she was away at a hotel for a Christmas break:

> In the dining room after breakfast on December 26, I overheard people talking in the next room, to the effect that the previous owners of the hotel had said 'Well... there is a strong scent of lavender sometimes'... just before 1 p.m. I went upstairs to my room – on the top floor of three, at the end of the house and through a fire door which left a small corridor with three rooms off it: one mine, one occupied by a young man of seventeen or so, one empty. There I was met with a *very* strong smell of lavender, no doubt of the scent. I thought it was probably due to some substance used in bathroom cleaning – they do tend to be overpowering – and

entered my room. No smell of anything in there (the bathroom cleaner was pine, by the way) my husband came into the room a couple of minutes later, by which time, the overheard conversation was beginning to have effect. 'Did you smell lavender in the corridor?' I said, 'No, not [...] lavender – a faint, sweet smell that's all.' After only two minutes [the] really strong smell, like perfume spilled on a carpet, say, had almost vanished, and in an unventilated small corridor too. Hmm. There was no frightening feeling of a 'presence', or if there was one it was quite friendly.

Others described a floral scent, again occurring at a time when they least expected it, and attributed it to being from an unexplainable, perhaps angelic source. Lorne Troop wrote 'although I have never seen an angel, I have experienced angel help and protection and I feel a loving presence near me as I work or whenever I travel. My mother and I are often aware of a beautiful fragrance.'

Some experiences seem more subtle, as David Lomax explained:

[I was] making my way home one evening from the local Tube station. It was still light but fairly early in the year, and I was surprised to catch a strong scent of flowers. Looking around for an explanation I could see no flowers but, on seeing two ladies not far behind me, reasoned that at least one had been a little extravagant in the application of perfume. However, as I made my way down the hill, the smell remained with me, even thought they had turned off. It fact it stayed with me for most of the fifteen minutes it took me to walk home. I was fairly nonplussed by this, but didn't really know what to make of it, and it was only some time later that I came across a book on angels, having started doing some reading in this subject, which mentioned the possibility that angels can 'appear' as scent. That really made me think and it was then that I made the connection, which had not struck me previously. Some month prior to this I had had an experience which I found equally bewildering. I don't know if you have come across the 'angel cards'... they feature qualities such as 'Love', 'Peace', 'Spontaneity', 'Creativity' etc... written in a calligraphic style and printed together with very attractive simple pictures in colour, all on a small card in a rectangular shape. I was most bemused to come across one of these cards on the pavement in a suburban street near my home, as it seemed a most unlikely thing to have dropped from anyone's pocket. I was intrigued to know who in the locality might be using such cards (often used as an aid to meditation or simply for inspiration), but adverts in local newsagents' windows elicited no response, and the card I found still sits facing me above the desk as I write. Having started to think about my other experience as an angelic one, I realised that the scent had disappeared at the spot where I found the card. This may be a fairly flimsy coincidence to most people, but it seemed a confirmation to me that I had been given some sort of message...

Others had similar unexpected experiences, often in their own home where the source could not be identified. Muriel Duffy wrote that, 'I have lived in my present home for thirty years – and sometimes, particularly when entering the dining room, there was [...] a very strong smell of pipe tobacco. As both my husband and I used to smoke cigarettes, it was odd the tobacco smell was so obvious (smoking dulls the sense of smell); no one else ever smelled it, and the last time I did I went into the dining room, noticed the aroma and said, "Oh hello, you are here again, are you!" Since then, no more tobacco smells.'

Scent and death

As we shall see in chapter nine, the vast majority of experiences of scent are in some way connected with death. Sometimes a scent is noticed a couple of weeks before a death, as Cecilia Blaikie noted of an incident that occurred shortly before her husband died: '[I] was awoken by a lovely fragrance which lasted for a few minutes. It happened again the following night.' She couldn't think what it was, 'but wished it had gone on and on!' Other experiences happened at the actual moment of death – a well-known and well-documented occurrence witnessed by many who are in the presence of the dying. I received the same amount of letters, however, from people who were not present at the death of a friend or relative, but who had this particular type of encounter at the precise moment of their death.

Many people wrote to me about the phenomenon of smelling flowers in the room at the precise time that someone passed away – 'an aroma of flowers at the moment our mother passed away'. One lady noticed 'a strong scent of lilies when my mother was dying, yet there weren't any flowers there'. As discussed in chapter five, it was the experience of smelling an intense perfume beside his mother's sickbed that alerted Michael Olden to the fact something was awry, and that same moment she unexpectedly passed away.

Jenny Jackson's husband was in hospital terminally ill and unable to communicate:

As I sat by the his bed surrounded by drips... and trying to say goodbye, I became aware of a scent of flowers. I had never actually been present at a death before, and asked his nurse if that was usual. She said no but that she could smell it too, was it her perfume? It wasn't. We both looked out of the window into a bare concrete yard full of oxygen cylinders – nothing there. I know it wasn't my imagination, as she smelt it too. At that time I didn't recognise the scent, but in October 1990 I went to see my husband's family in Australia and in a remote village in Western Australia I smelt the smell again – it was honeysuckle – my husband's favourite flower for scent. I have always believed that this was his way of saying goodbye to me.

Rita King wrote that on the death of her father in hospital and the death of her mother in her own home, she experienced 'an overwhelming scent of flowers on both occasions'. Lavinia Bradley told me how '[my husband]... died with me, but when the undertakers came to take him away, I couldn't bear it and went out into the garden. I didn't come in until they had driven away with him. I went to the empty room and was deluged in a sweet floral scent, almost like an embrace. For an instant I almost felt this was some sort of last gesture from him, then reasoned I was being ridiculous and that probably [the] undertakers used some sort of freshener. To this day I have never asked if this is their practice because, fantastic though it, I [want] to believe it was something from him.'

A very similar thing happened to Carol Thomas after her mother had suddenly passed away while she was visiting her:

After paramedics, doctors and undertakers had completed their formalities, my father and I went to see her for the last time, laid out on the guest bed. I was immediately struck by a strong odour of flowers. It was not really natural and I had not smelt it before. I tended to think it was how the body had been prepared... even when they took her away and after a further two nights when my father slept in there, that same smell pervaded the room, although no one else was particularly aware of it.

We then decided to take my father back to his house... when we arrived I needed something out of a case which had been put on the guest bed upstairs. As I opened the door, I was literally knocked backwards by an extremely pungent scent – flower-like – and instinctively said 'Oh, hello Mum!' [The smell was also smelt again in her father's lounge where Carol's mother used to sit.]

At the time of Eric Dyson's mother's death in 1947, Eric, his father and brother were in the living room when they all noticed 'a very heavy, sweet scent of flowers which lasted for only a few moments but was very definite'. His mother was at the time very ill in hospital. 'She had always told us that she would not have wallflowers (she was very specific about this) in the house as their scent had been noticed before her own mother's death... I can confirm this as a true account of our experience but have no explanation for it other than an angelic visitation.'

Patricia Fountain wrote:

A neighbour of my mother's, her official carer and on whom she depended on absolutely, died after a short illness. I woke in the morning, in my own home, and the bedroom was pervaded by what I can only

describe as a flowery perfume, or potpourri. I do not
have flowers or other such things in the bedroom. I
even asked my husband if he had changed his
aftershave. I gave no more thought to it until later that
evening when I had a call from the neighbour's son to
tell me of his mother's death and asking me to break
the news to my mother.

Harry Lovelock had a similar experience at a time when one of
his friends was dying from cancer:

I was visiting my daughter in Leicestershire, the
weather cold and my bedroom bare of flowers or any
kind of perfume. I woke at 3:20 a.m. aware of a strong,
heady, pleasing aroma and I sat up, fully awake,
switched on my bedside lamp and looked around the
room, this time breathing in deeply in an attempt to
ensure I wasn't imagining things. After a time I lay
back feeling comforted but unable to explain why. I
drove back to London after breakfast and, switching
on my answering machine, heard the young woman's
husband say that my friend had died, in the hospice,
at 3:25 that morning.

Dr Ernst's wife died on October 16 1998 after suffering from
cancer of the lung. He wrote:

We had a truly wonderful marriage for thirty-three
years of love, laughter and total happiness. During the
last few months I do not think two people could have
been closer than we were. We had been able to
discuss our lives together, but most important of all,
we were able to say 'Goodbye', and each give our

permission for the other to let go. We both had faith and were practising members of the Church of England. Neither of us were psychic, although we often knew what the other was thinking. I think this was due to having a close marriage with good communication.

On the night of October 16 I went to bed at about 10 p.m. and fell into a deep sleep. About 3 a.m. I woke up, and the room was full of the scent of roses. I called out to see if she was there, but I heard and saw nothing. I was at all times totally awake and tried to find the source of this wonderful aroma, but there was nothing in the house or garden remotely like it. The experience lasted about twenty minutes.

Several people wrote to me to recount their experience of smelling a particular scent on a number of occasions some time after the death of a loved one. Mrs Archer told me that she has '... had the wonderful experience of smelling a perfume, so beautiful – a real bouquet of flowers. This has [happened] four times on anniversaries of my mum's death...'

Maggy Brook wrote of '... a curious incident which occurred when I was twelve...'

My mother died of kidney disease and my father (a devout Christian) arranged for the funeral service to be held in our sitting room. My mother was a Roman Catholic but never ever set foot in a church...
The coffin was in the room for two to three days and afterwards there was an overpowering smell of spring flowers there, in fact I would often just go in to smell them... it is only in later years I realise this was a very strange phenomenon – I mean, if I move a pot of

hyacinths out of my room the smell won't linger more than a day – how on earth can it stay a year or so?

'On the day in which my dear wife died at 5 a.m.,' wrote Mr Winepress, 'as I lay in bed the room was suddenly filled with an overpowering smell of flowers, although there weren't any in the house, this also happened on the following two nights.' A similar occurrence: '... when my mother died. For about three months after her death I was aware of the same kind of floral perfume in different parts of the house and at different times of day. It did not happen anywhere else.'

When Margaret's brother died, she 'soon afterwards... experienced a wonderful scent throughout the house, which was corroborated by friends who came to help and can only be described as "down to earth". The perfume was obvious but so delicate, and in spite of the deep sorrow I felt at Sandy's passing, there was the most wonderful feeling of peace.'

On the day Rosalie Double's 'dear mother died in 1952, I too, experienced an intense scent of fresh flowers – all separate and identifiable. No one else in the family could smell them and when I realised it could be a message from my mother it was cut off immediately and as suddenly as the shutting of a door, as if once the message of incomparable beauty had got through to me, that was sufficient.'

Oseni Lawal lost one of his childhood friends when he was eighteen. A Muslim, Oseni 'prayed fervently that he may go to heaven. I prayed alone in an open space/yard. After a couple of minutes of praying, I sensed a sweet smell of flowers around me of whose origin I could not tell. My belief then was that it was my friend who was present in sprit just to say "all is well". As if to say "your prayer is answered and I am now peacefully at rest in heaven"... It could as well have been a visitation from an angel to indicate that my prayer had been answered.'

Mrs Fleming's experience followed her mother's unexpected death back in March 1969. 'Having dashed down from the Welsh border to the New Forest and tried to comfort my father, I felt I would never sleep that night. As I lay in the dark the most exquisite scent of flowers filled the room – better than hyacinths, lilies or orange blossom but similar – it really was like nothing I have ever smelt before or since. I felt a great sense of comfort, and fell into a dreamless sleep and woke quite refreshed to face the day.'

On the day Margaret Kemp-Lewis's mother had died in hospital she was driving back home on her own. Suddenly the car was filled with the sweet scent of flowers, and although I didn't understand why I knew it had to be connected with her death. It's something I will never forget and I feel very privileged to have had that experience.'

Mrs Sharman wrote about an experience both she and her daughter had: '… my daughter had a little girl, stillborn. It was after that we both experienced a strong smell of roses in two different rooms in two different houses. This was most strange and needless to say I searched the room for evidence of the smell but found nothing. It happened once to us both and is something we will never forget.'

After the death of 'a very dear friend' of Mrs Cooper's she entered the bedroom and there was a 'very strong perfume of flowers…', then, 'a few weeks after my husband passed away, I entered the hall of my flat, the smell of perfume was terrific. It was quite scary, it happened again but this time was very slight. It really is quite a mystery.'

An elderly lady friend of Mrs Marsh had lost her son as a result of a lorry knocking him off his bicycle '… she said that following his death, she experienced a beautiful, calming sensation of flowers throughout her bedroom in the middle of the night. She then felt 'at peace' and has always felt it could have been a floral 'message' of some sort'.

'On three occasions,' Mrs Archer wrote, she has '... had the strong smell of tobacco and cinnamon, which was definitely my dad, but was never noticed by my husband.'

ANGELS OF MERCY

'Suddenly through my tears I saw what I thought to be a figure, an angel, behind the bed rails – I ignored it, thinking it was exhaustion and anxiety. A few minutes later I looked to see my son staring at the same spot – he turned to me and asked if I too could see an angel behind the bed...'

WHAT ALL THE following experiences have in common is the fact that they each took place during a time of illness and provided the recipient with strength and support. These accounts happened to those who were seriously ill, and to their loved ones. The section 'Angels in Waiting' below examines experiences surrounding the terminally ill and dying and then leads on to experiences that happened specifically within a hospital – whether to a member of staff, patient or visitor.

David Jacobs was literally waiting for death after having been told that he had an enlarged heart that was already 90% dead and kidneys that had suffered complete renal failure with high toxin levels:

> At the age of fifty-four I was still desperate to earn a living as a self-employed artist – there were three young children to bring up and [I] had no savings to fall back on so I was still travelling to the Bayswater Road Art Show every Sunday. I had gone to bed at around ten o'clock and for four hours slept soundly. At two o'clock I was conscious of a great light in the room and a 'presence'.
>
> An angel was sitting at the foot of the bed with a wing stretched out in front of me. Beyond it I could see and hear large numbers of my family who had passed on, calling to me from the vestibule of what seemed like an old cinema.
>
> I could not make out the sex of the angel but it was the most beautiful creature I had ever seen. It was probably twice my height and pulsated love and golden light into the room. It said nothing, but when I

attempted to move towards my mother and my late brother Derek, I felt the outstretched wing holding me back. From that moment I knew I would not die. Within a few seconds I knew it had lost its brilliance and it was gone.

Since then I have received a heart transplant... and gone back to selling my paintings... I intend to keep working for the rest of my life so that I can, in some small way, help others or find whatever it was that I have been spared for.

Mary, now writing over 70 years since the event she describes, told me of a story her mother relayed to her, although there are parts of her experience that still remain with her to this day. Aged three, Mary was seriously ill with double pneumonia and not expected to live through the night – her mother was in the next room, extremely distraught, preparing Mary's white dress to wrap her dead body in when the time came. However, she was disturbed when Mary apparently called out that there was a fairy in the corner of her room. She can still remember the marvellous feeling of happiness and hearing 'beautiful music, like no other music she had ever heard' when she saw the figure, but 'unfortunately can not recall details about him/her, except that a red corded girdle was worn [which at the time reminded her of a tie-back to a curtain they had!], and a long robe.' From this moment Mary began to recover and had the first good night's sleep she had had in weeks. The doctor arrived the next morning, amazed she was not only still alive, but in almost perfect health.

In August 1994, Effie Devenish had spent a week in hospital with an erratic heartbeat. On her return home she was, naturally, very weary, so she booked herself into a Christian guesthouse in Groombridge.

One day I was at the washbasin in my room when I glanced up into the mirror. Behind my left shoulder I saw, very clearly, a figure in white, which I later assumed to be an angel. When I glanced away and then back again, the figure had gone. At first I thought it to be a trick of the light, but no way during the rest of my stay did I see the figure again. I had been feeling depressed and frightened as a result of my heart trouble, but after the visitation I felt quite differently – weary, but relaxed and no longer afraid. I then felt quite convinced that this angel had been sent to me to care for me and protect me from my fears.

Jean Arnold wrote:

My experience is a little different from those I read about. I have MS and am confined to a wheelchair. I used to go to a 'healing' lady (she didn't accept the words 'faith healer') for relaxation. One day about a year ago I, as she used to call it, 'let go' – this is like being in a very relaxed state. Suddenly a man, about 5 foot 9 inches tall, with brown hair and with brown hair round his face (not a beard), was standing in front of me. There was a belt or tie around his waist and he was wearing sandals. All at once he was gone and my lady friend was standing where he had been.

I said, 'There was a man standing there just now.' She replied, 'It was your guardian angel.' She was so pleased for me. The experience has never reoccurred since [and I had never experienced] anything previously. I can still see him clearly to this day

Helen Murphy's husband had undergone major surgery:

We knew that a further operation was likely if recommended by the surgeon, but I had already accepted that he was terminally ill, although I had no idea of the time scale beyond...

It was during this period... before the second operation that I had my angel experience. At the time it happened I thought that I was awake, but in the morning it seemed like more of a dream and may well have been so, though this does not invalidate the experience. I was lying in bed with my husband asleep beside me. At the foot of bed two figures appeared, one male (standing on the left, on my husband's side) and one female (standing on the right on my side). They were dressed alike in white, short-sleeved jackets (with a round neck and buttoned across the shoulder and down the side) worn over dark trousers. The general effect was vaguely medical – definitely no wings and halos! They stood silent with arms by their sides, then slowly walked around the bed to stand facing each other, the male by my husband the female by me. No words were spoken, and they remained there for what seemed like some minutes before fading away. They were not threatening, but certainly very serious in their aspect. I was in no doubt that they were our guardian angels who had come to indicate their support for the difficult time ahead. In the morning, I knew then that he was going to die.

The second operation was not a success and her husband died a few weeks later.

Norma Gallagher's late mother saw an angel early one morning while she was sitting up in bed drinking a cup of tea in her bedroom. Apparently the angel entered her room and stood in the doorway, looking at her – she described it as being 'very bright and beautiful with shimmering wings'. Shortly after the experience she was taken ill with leukaemia, and always thought that the angel had come to give her strength to accept the dreadful illness. As Norma points out, although her mother passed away in 1985 she will always remember her mum's angel and the help and comfort she received from the visitation.

Angels in waiting

Some respondents reported seeing an angel quietly standing (or perhaps waiting) beside the dying before they passed away, whereas others have witnessed many examples of 'bright glowing light in the presence of the dying', in the words of one respondent, Julie Baxter. Sometimes these experiences happened a matter of weeks before the inevitable death or just moments before the sufferer slipped away. From this the witnesses took great comfort and strength, seeing it as a sign that their loved one would be looked after. When Diane Davie's husband was dying of cancer, she '… came home, went to the lounge room and saw a seven-foot angel standing behind his chair with "her" wings wrapped around him. [Her husband] was sleeping peacefully (unusual). Very real… big, white gown, white wings, golden face, brown eyes full of love (I had eye contact) – the angel was glowing with a golden light.'

Mrs Jordan described how she saw an angel many years ago during the war when she was visiting her music teacher, who lived with her brother:

> I was leaving the house and said I would see myself
> out when – to my shock – an angel covered the door
> I had to open. It had beautiful, outstretched wings, a
> man's face. I eventually plucked up courage and
> opened the door to return home. I mentioned this

encounter to a friend – a spiritualist – who said it was
the angel of death and only visited very good people.

Two days after seeing the angel I had a phone call
to say that my teacher's brother had suddenly died
and would I visit her. I did go and mentioned the
angel and she said it was there when she went to bed
that night, so I know I hadn't imagined it. I am now
eighty-three and can still see this encounter...

Finally, one gentleman wrote with an account told to him by
his grandmother. On November 20th 1895, her six-and-a-half-
year-old son lay ill and told his mother that he could see angels
at the foot of his sick bed. He waved to them and said, 'I am
coming tomorrow.' The little boy died the following day...

Hospital angels

A staggering 9.5% of recipients recounted that their
experiences took place in hospital – these visitations were
made either to people on their sickbed, those enduring a long
or painful illness, or to those keeping vigil who felt or saw an
angelic presence in the room. This chapter shares many
similarities with the chapters ten ('Twilight Experiences') and
nine ('Angels of Death'), although the following experiences
have happened to people specifically around hospital or
sickbeds. Some outline personal experiences from the
recipients, others report observations of the sick from other
patients on the ward or relatives who were sat with them.

Last Christmas I had to spend a night in the local hospital.
During my stay one of the nurses recognised me from some
publicity about this work that was being circulated in the
media at that time. Word soon spread and the surly looking
consultant, whilst doing his rounds came over – looked around
the ward and almost whispered, 'There must be hundreds of

them in here – I've personally never seen one but I'm sure some of the patients can – we hear stories all the time.' That night, admittedly, angels were furthest from my mind, but after that comment, I did begin to people-watch as the hours slowly passed. Patients with all sorts of complaints in the mixed admissions ward surrounded me. One lady opposite kept crying out to an invisible something at the side of her bed; another gentleman's eyes were fixed on the far corner of the ceiling. There are plenty of possible explanations for such behaviour, drugs and fatigue being among the most obvious ones. But that night, whether there were angels present or not, the comments I received only highlighted the strong sense of belief in angels of death, or angels of comfort, held by many nursing staff and doctors.

Many of the replies I received to my request for accounts of encounters with angels were written by doctors or nurses. The following account was from a palliative care nurse who had been working alongside Mr and Mrs X – Mr X had been admitted to hospital after being diagnosed with an incurable disease. The doctors were optimistic that treatment might slow down the disease process and improve his symptoms, so the nurse had a lot of contact over the next few weeks with Mr and Mrs X, both by telephone and in the outpatients department.

At the beginning of [November] Mr X became acutely ill at home and was taken to the A&E department with a condition unrelated to his previous diagnosis. He was admitted to hospital and, despite active treatment, his condition deteriorated over the next few days and I was heavily involved in advising about his symptom management and providing psychological support for the family.

On the morning of... [his death], I had a message

to say that Mr X had just died, he had been comfortable and his family had been at his bedside. The family were still on the ward and asked if I could go down and see them, which I did.

I left the ward at the same time as the trolley taking Mr X's body to the mortuary. I held the doors open to let the porters take the trolley through, and I followed them down the corridor until they stopped at the lifts. As I walked past I brushed my hand lightly against the side of the trolley and thought 'Goodbye Mr X' and continued walking towards the stairs.

Next to the lifts is a stairwell that staff generally use, rather than waste time waiting for the lifts. It is always busy and even if you don't see anyone you can usually hear doors banging, people chatting, bleeps etc. The building has seven floors, and I joined the stairwell on the third floor to go to the wards on the sixth floor.

As I went through the doors I noted it was *very* quiet, with none of the usual hustle/bustle and buzz. My thoughts turned away completely to a situation totally unrelated to work that was worrying me (I can remember *exactly* what I was thinking about). Suddenly I became aware of a feeling of stillness, with no sense of time/sound/space and everything seemed both incredibly intense but also very nebulous...

As I became more aware of these feelings, I felt that I was contained in a beam of clear white light that went the whole height and almost the whole width of the building (and I was about halfway up). Then I *sensed* (rather than saw) a pair of enormous wings coming around from the back of the beam of light, completely enfolding me and I *knew* it was an angelic being. I was overwhelmed with emotion and an amazing sense of safety/protection/love/compassion, and I felt both very calm and yet incredibly elated.

And then, as soon as I tried to focus on what was happening, it was gone as quickly as it had come. I suddenly felt myself being dragged back – I felt dense and heavy, could hear noises and felt temperature. My overriding feeling at that stage was that, for however long it was – time had stood still, almost – that I'd stepped into another dimension to have this experience...

Later, when I had time to think about this experience, I wasn't really able to make any more of it, other than I know it did happen... I've been up and down those same stairs every working day since then – without a hint of any sensations or experiences...

Joanie was one of the first people I ever spoke with about angels. In fact, our very meeting could be classed as one of those weird episodes some would call fate, others coincidence – all I can say is if it hadn't been for some of the things Joanie told me during our first conversation, then I don't think the original idea for finding out more about angelic visitations would ever have seriously entered my head. She has seen angels around people since her early childhood and has vividly explained to me how the hospice where she works as an auxiliary nurse is 'packed with angels' – especially standing beside the dying. Joanie wrote:

Working [at the] hospice it is truly a privilege to sit with someone as they approach the end of their life. What I have experienced and understood since I was small is that we all have a guardian angel, who is with you always from the moment you are born.

There was one night in the hospice [when] a lady was struggling for breath, having lung cancer [...] must be one of the most frightening ways to die. As I sat with her, I felt a presence at the foot of her bed; slowly, a young girl of about seven years gradually emerged wearing a lovely pink frock. She gazed at the lady with such love; also, to the back of the bed, appeared two angels with huge wings (one was her guardian angel). They were waiting to guide her on her journey. The lady suddenly opened her eyes and as she saw the girl a calmness enveloped her. She then took her last breath. After such a long, hard struggle with her disease there was peace all around.

It transpired, unknown to me, that she had lost a daughter aged seven and never got over it. It seemed a great healing process had occurred in that moment. No one is alone, you are surrounded by angels and loved ones constantly.

Birth and angels

Having a baby is one of the most traumatic yet wonderful experiences in any woman's life, so it is hardly surprising so many letters came in relating otherworldly experiences associated with this moment. Two letters recounted stories from the respondents' own mothers about their births. June Helps wrote that her mother 'has always been so sure about the fact that when I was about to be born – she saw an angel in her room – "it" had wonderfully white wings and vanished into the wardrobe. The matron in the nursing home told my mother it was her guardian angel. We have always laughed at the fact it vanished into the wardrobe, but my mother has steadfastly said over the years [that] she didn't dream it she saw it and [that] it was wonderful – we always put it down to the stress of childbirth as she was only twenty at the time.'

Terence Wynn's mother was a professional gymnast who had taken time out for his birth at her sister-in-law's home while the other members of her act continued their tour of theatres under the management of his father. She too had a 'visitation' toward the end of her pregnancy on November 20 1928:

I was late, having been due in early October and the doctor was concerned because I was going to be a big baby and my mother was a small woman. She wrote to my father each night, reassuring him that all was well when she herself was deeply concerned...

She was a very organised lady and kept a notebook at her bedside to record any event involving herself physically or an idea to be pursued later. This evening, shortly before midnight, she was finishing her letter to my dad when she thought her sister-in-law had come into the room where she was finishing the scribe. 'I'm sorry if I kept you up Laura, but I'm just closing this letter to Derek', she said as she signed off. When she looked up [she] saw a young man in a white gown – almost translucent but solid – at the bottom of the bed, holding a baby in his arms. The child was about six months old with a dimple in its right cheek. The man smiled and pointed to the baby and said 'it won't be long'. Then, still smiling, he moved away and through the French windows into the garden and my mother says he walked up the garden path and then disappeared. He seemed to glide, the baby was on his back, looking back at her.

She immediately wrote all this down in her notebook, which I still possess... One week later, shortly before midnight, I was born after a difficult birth and the first thing my mother said to the midwife was 'Has the baby got a dimple on his right cheek?' The midwife was astonished. 'Yes, how did you know that?' My mother said simply 'I know because I met him a week ago.'

My mother died eight years ago at the age of ninety and she maintained to the end that what she had seen was true.'

After about the seventh false alarm before the birth of Eileen Wilson's fourth child, she was at last in hospital having 'been bathed and lying on a high bed with a bell given me as it was lunchtime and the doctor's visit due...'

I am viewing the high ceiling, large room and ornate corners of the white ceiling. The baby was about to be born – not as expected via the nurse on her examination – I'd reached back for the bell and lost it – it swung to and fro and I could not reach for it to press. I lay there and distantly heard trolleys (lunch) and distant feet. I [tried to] take my mind off the pain – I thought of names and recall saying 'If it's a girl I'll have mother's name, Mary!' plus I called on Jesus Christ to help me. I'd called for help (nurse) to no avail. I heard a 'swishing' noise – like wind – and behold I was lifted up to a sitting position. How, you may ask. Via what I can only describe as [...] a hand and arm to above elbow. Its strength took all my weight, keeping me level and balanced and sitting upright. Its strength held me on my right arm, just above my elbow. I recall flopping backwards and in came the nurse, utterly surprised and I was hurriedly wheeled into the delivery room... my own doctor at the time said he would not dispute this, as he'd heard so much in his time as a doctor. No one else believed me, I'm sure...

When she experienced an angelic visitation, Jean Gallager 'knew he was not of this world, yet I accepted him quite naturally, fascinated by the fact that he had no feet and seemed to be suspended about twelve inches above the floor on which I lay. He had a serene sensitive face, full of compassion, yet smiling and kind...'

'Don't be afraid' he said smiling at me. 'Your time is not yet come.' Even the words came from another age, and I was enveloped in a most wonderful calm and peaceful tranquillity, as he slowly faded away. The white rough cloth gown that was so real, I felt I could touch it, fading to muslin, to gauze and finally gone.
I lay there at peace, after the trauma of the last twenty-four hours, when I had been pushed from the labour room of the local cottage hospital after the woman in the next bed had delivered a dead baby and died herself.

In the resultant confusion, a harassed nurse pushed me into an adjoining bathroom, saying, 'You shouldn't be seeing all this.'

Dawn was breaking – suddenly there was activity all around me as the nurses swaddled me in bright red blankets, and two ambulance men stretchered me down narrow stairs to a waiting ambulance and we were off at an alarming pace, with the ambulance bell ringing away above our heads. There was a great sense of unreality. Hadn't my guardian angel told me all would be well?

It was a frosty morning, crisp and very cold. The sky was blue, and the tops of the trees were black patterns painted with white frost against the blue sky. I lay still – at peace. Doors opened and closed, more noise, more people and then quiet again. I opened my eyes again, My bed was surrounded by people, all dressed in green – like Martians I thought – green gowns, green close-fitting matching hats covering every strand of hair; and why were they wearing gloves?

As I looked at them I was amazed to see them fold their hands in prayer, their leader, at the foot of my bed, closed her eyes and as she started to pray I felt a prick on the back of my hand, and they slowly faded away. And then anther pressure on my hand, and a voice saying, 'You have a perfect baby girl.'

Over the years I often thought of the one I called my guardian angel. His face remained, and still does to this day, so vivid to me. And then one day – this is hard to believe, but is true – I saw that same face looking at me from the page of a book. I was so overwhelmed: the face now had a name. He couldn't be my guardian angel – he was living on this earth until I was seventeen years old. I discovered that he was born in Scotland – that in 1927, aged twenty-five, he emigrated to the United States and before long began working towards [a] ministerial career.

Within nineteen years he had risen to be Chaplain of the United States Senate. His sincerity together with his gifts as a public speaker made him well known and greatly loved. He died, at the height of his power and popularity, in 1949. He was forty-six years old.

I was so happy to discover his identity, and I read everything I could lay my hands on, to learn more about him. I felt that I knew him so well and I was happy that he was able to carry on his ministry, for that was surely what his visit to me meant.

And then, there was an even stranger coincidence! In researching our family tree, some cousins sent me photocopies of all they had found and yes, unbelievable though it sounds, there was the name of that 'angel'. We were the same bloodline from the same root of that family in Scotland so long ago.

It was after giving birth that Sylvia Gower had her angelic experience. For over eleven years Sylvia and her husband had been trying for a child; then, after unsuccessfully journeying down the various avenues of adoption, they moved to a smaller house where she fell pregnant. Because of her blood pressure she was persuaded to have new treatment, which entailed having to accept going into hospital for the last three weeks and be prepared to have a Caesarean birth:

When I came round, I was in another small room. A nurse said, 'You've got a baby daughter. She weighed 4lbs 8oz.' She was in the intensive care unit – I'd be taken to see her later. I don't remember my emotions as I first saw this tiny baby. She had wires attached to her body. They seemed to be everywhere. I put my hand into the incubator – her little finger curled round mine. Her grip was surprisingly tight. I immediately loved her.

Reluctantly, I was taken back to my room – eager to see her the next day. Before we went to the baby unit next, I was warned that she had developed a bit of jaundice. This often happened with premature babies. When I entered the baby unit, the wires had been removed. As I looked into her tiny face, a doubt crept into my mind. I immediately thrust it aside. Back in my room, I spoke to no one about my thoughts.

But, by the following day, I could no longer deny my doubts. This dear little soul had Down's Syndrome. The obstetrician came round when I was back in my room – he asked me how I felt. I replied I was depressed because the room was still cluttered with post-op apparatus. I think he guessed. Later they sent for my husband, so we could see the hospital paediatrician together.

When my husband arrived I broke down and told him my fears... After my husband [went] that evening, leaving me alone, I wept and wept. A different nurse popped her head around the door (the regular ones seemed to be avoiding me, having offered me a 'happy pill', which I had refused). She said she'd been sent to borrow a piece of equipment for the top ward. Listening to my story between my sobs, she sat on the bed and held me in her arms. [She told me] she had a sister with a child like mine and what joy he brought to the family. She stayed a long time talking until I had calmed down. It never occurred to me how she would account for her long absence. Her name was stitched on her uniform – 'Nurse White'. She helped me get things into perspective – the little baby that we already felt immense love for was still the same, regardless of this new tag. It just meant she would need extra love and care.

So, when she weighed 5lbs we were allowed to take our daughter home to the room we had prepared for

her. Of course, it was not easy – and never would be –
but thanks to Nurse White, I had been given the
courage to meet the challenge.

A few months later, after her christening, we went
back to the baby unit to take the caring staff there
some cake. I also took a piece for Nurse White, but
when I went with it, no one seemed to know her…
Only recently, reading stories from people who are
sure they have been helped by angels, have I
remembered that night and the difference she made.
Whether Nurse White was a nurse or an angel, I'm
very glad of her visit twenty-five years ago.[1]

Angelic visitations to patients

Anver Hajee had been rushed into hospital with sudden chest
pains. 'I was walking back from the office and I had a slight
pain and I was rushed into hospital. In three days the QE [the
local hospital] decided to operate on me because they said you
are absolutely blocked, we have to operate [on] you…'
Terrified in the knowledge both his father and brother had
died at 32 and 48 respectively from heart attacks, Anver
underwent an angiogram that revealed three of his arteries
were blocked. He was put on a drip and told to move as little
as possible before his emergency surgery the following day. 'I
have a child who has cerebral palsy,' he revealed, 'and I love her
very much. I thought, if I die I will leave her behind. Fear was
in my heart.' Then he went to the washroom and a figure
appeared behind the locked door. 'I was really frightened
because everything was happening so fast and I just couldn't
come to a conclusion of what I should do, whether I should
sign the consent [for the operation to go ahead] or not… in
the washroom I tried to get up – there's a handrail which you're
supposed to hold… and I couldn't get up on my feet…

Suddenly I saw this tall figure... seven [or] seven and a half feet, in white with [a] very pinkish face, long beard. It's the kind of image I have of Jesus Christ (I am a Muslim, an Asian)... and I saw this and the person tells me, "Take care, take care" and I felt the warmth on my hand, and he picked me up [...] I told the nurse a little bit but I was all confused, I just couldn't believe it. After that I signed all the papers and I went through the operation...'[2] What was particularly strange about Anver's experience is, as he explained, 'We speak Katchi at home, but he spoke to me in English.' Anver believes this Jesus figure was indeed his own guardian angel.

Barbara Parsons was in hospital, the night prior to undergoing an examination for a possible tumour. She was playing angel music (new-age relaxation tapes) and saying affirmation when 'from behind the bed and through the wall came a soft "cushing" noise which moved through me and the bed and filled the small room with golden light. I felt electric and spoke aloud: "It's you, you're here." I simply "knew" without a doubt that I was experiencing an angelic visitation. It lasted only a few minutes, then went back through me and the bed and the wall behind me. I didn't see with my eyes faces, or wings, but every atom of me knew what it was.' An aside: the consultant was sure Barbara had a tumour but on cystoscopy they found nothing there to account for her previous symptoms.

Angel encounters seem to happen in all situations in and around the hospital, as we have seen, to staff and patients before an operation such as Anver's and Barbara's and also after surgery, as was the case with Eric Walton. Eric was in hospital for an aortic embolism repair:

I was told if I didn't have this operation I would die but had a fifty-fifty chance of surviving the operation.

I decided to have the operation. Apparently it was a major operation and I was in theatre for some six and a half hours. [While I was] recovering in an intensive care ward, a lady appeared with white hair to her shoulders, with a white face and wearing a long white dress to the floor. She didn't smile but stood quite still half-looking at me. I spoke to her but got no reply. The vision was still there when my wife visited but she was unable to see the vision despite my insisting that she was there. I guess she stayed for about half an hour, strangely silent with a sort of Mona Lisa smile on her face. My wife and the doctors said I was hallucinating but I believe the vision was there to see me through my recovery. She hadn't come to take me away but to watch over my recovery.

A similar experience was recounted by Tony Hughes:

I can recall approximately twenty-five years ago when my father had just experienced a heart attack and he lay quite ill for several days without really acknowledging any of the family, upon regaining full consciousness said that he had witnessed a vivid image of an angel smiling at him through a bright light. Later, when he had made a full recovery, he again made reference to this experience.

I remember both these occasions well because I was surprised both then and now to hear my father, who was a well-educated man with a sound academic brain, talk of such things. I have to say that, at the time, all the family were practising Catholics and we frequently included in our private and group prayers the following:

Angel of God my guardian dear
To whom God's love put me here.
Ever this night stay by my side
To light and guard to rule and guide. Amen.

Interestingly, within recent years the Catholic Church has somewhat distanced itself from the notion of a guardian angel. However, I still pray to my guardian angel!

Janet Slaughter, a district nursing sister, 'suffered an acute illness affecting my pancreas and was quite ill in hospital for three days, and gradually improved with treatment. On the fourth or fifth day I was moved on to the main ward and that night had difficulty getting to sleep...

I tried hiding my head under the covers to block out the night-light in the centre of the ward but suddenly saw the light become brighter and move towards me. It was bright white/yellow and moving quite steadily. Then I was aware of the light under the bedclothes and my body felt very warm and was being shaken/vibrated. This lasted for a few seconds, only to be repeated again a few minutes later. This second time I had a feeling I was being helped in some way and murmured, 'Thank you, thank you'. As you may imagine I was not able to sleep for the rest of the night! Afterwards I had various tests and examinations but no cause for my illness was found and I have been perfectly well since.

A similar 'light experience' happened to Brian Martin when he was ill in 1979:

I was twenty-eight at the time... I fell very ill with food poisoning and was rushed into hospital intensive care and isolation for two weeks. It wasn't until afterwards I thought I was very close to death. I spent some time recovering at home and one night I was lying in bed and I cannot tell if I was asleep but I remember having my arm loosely hanging from the bed straight to the outside edge. Suddenly a brilliant white light passed from the bottom of the bed and touched my arm, which felt like a very fine silky material, and immediately passed through the wall at the head of the bed, and was gone in a split second. I felt no fear only a deep peace and a reassurance that all was well and that I had been saved from danger.

Elizabeth MacMaster wrote, 'My fourteen-year-old son was dying and in the final distressing stage of leukaemia. When he was almost too weak to talk he said quite clearly that two angels had stood at the foot of his hospital bed. Though ethics mattered in my family, we had never expressed religious beliefs nor talked of angels.'

Another lady who wrote to me, described how she had visited an elderly lady friend who had been hospitalised for a leg wound. She maintained that her friend 'was not senile or mentally wandering' though she spoke of how 'she knew others in the ward were about to die as shortly before they had done so she had seen an angel standing by their bedside.'

Other stories are similar but vary in that it is not the fellow patients who 'see' the angel; instead, they notice a strange behaviour in the dying before they pass away. Mrs. Marsh wrote about a time she was in hospital recovering from an operation when an elderly lady was brought in with a blood clot in her leg:

Her very serious condition meant that the nurses had to constantly treat her. Throughout the second night she kept raising herself up, arms outstretched towards the bottom of her bed then shaking her head and sinking back down in great pain. As she was keeping myself, and indeed the whole ward awake, I was watching her throughout that night and wondering if indeed she was being 'called' by an angel(s) but fighting for her life here. In the morning the screens were put around her and she had passed away.

An identical story came from another lady who, with a friend, was visiting an elderly lady in hospital who kept 'raising her head and pointing to the end of her bed as if acknowledging someone [...] I am totally convinced there were angels there.' She too died twenty-four hours later.

Angelic visitations to non-patients
The accounts written by those who had been visiting a patient in hospital and had had an angelic experience shared a common theme: the experiences all seemed to revolve around the issue of death, something we shall explore more fully in the following chapter.

When Roessa Chivesman's mother died in hospital, she saw 'a shaft of bright light sloping from above and down to her' and attributed this to a possible angelic presence or force.

Anthea Lang's mother had been unconscious for over three days in hospital:

We had a call from the hospital informing us her condition had deteriorated. We had been sitting with her for about six hours prior to the call and had returned home briefly for a short rest. On returning to the hospital about 6:30 p.m. we found a nurse sitting, holding my mother's hand. My mother was still unconscious but the nurse told us she didn't like anyone to die alone. We sat for a few further hours, during which time there had been absolutely no change in my mother's condition. Whilst the hospital corridor was brightly lit, only a dim light was switched on in the room. We went into the corridor for about one minute, during which time we decided we'd stay at the hospital all night if necessary. We then returned to the room. Immediately it was apparent that something indefinable was happening. My mother's condition had altered – quite how I could not immediately decide – and I became aware that something was in the room with us. I felt the presence of an angel dressed in black. Oddly, my husband also felt a presence in the room. We called a nurse, who realised my mother was at the point of death. After a horrible illness... my mother suddenly seemed comforted.

After, when we talked about this, we felt that my mother had wanted us to leave the room when we did – she felt she could not die with others present. I have spoken to others about this and understand it is quite a common feeling. I am convinced she was visited by at least one angel during our absence from the room...

Mary Huntly spent the last week of her husband's life permanently at his side in hospital back in 1986. For two years he had been in a 'waking coma', and during his final few days Mary was allowed to stay with him all the time, night and day. But, she said, 'there was another presence there with us, which I can only describe as the Angel of the Presence of God...'

He stood, motionless, yet vibrant in immense power, and I felt he was there to ease the passing of my husband and to assure me that he was going to be healed by death into life with God.

Although he was larger than a human man and dressed in a white... robe, there was no fear at all in my perception of him, just a total impression of a loving, caring, supportive presence of enormous power and love. I am sure he was sent to strengthen and protect us both at a very crucial time.

I shall conclude this chapter with one of the experiences I have perhaps spoken most about in the varying publicity surrounding this project. One lady was in the intensive care unit following a routine hysterectomy that had had serious complications due to an allergy to the anaesthetic. Unexpectedly called in, her husband and son sat at her bedside while she lay there unconscious:

Suddenly, through my tears, I saw what I thought to be a figure, an angel, behind the bed rails – I ignored it, thinking it was [brought about by] exhaustion and anxiety. A few minutes later I looked to see my son staring at the same spot – he turned to me and asked if I too could see an angel behind the bed. That moment the staff nurse was passing the foot of the bed and I turned and asked her if she could see anything other than us in the cubicle – the nurse smiled and told us not to presume it meant the worst. She acted as if this was a normal occurrence. I turned back to my wife and watched the figure melt away. Literally from that moment on my wife regained consciousness.

ANGELS OF DEATH

'I was going to see my father who was in the intensive
care unit at the hospital. As I went into the room... I saw
my mother sitting on the right-hand side of my father,
then my eyes were drawn to the left-hand side and there I
could see an angel in shining apparel. He was shining a
silvery colour from head to toe and his wings really stood
out to me, they were feathered and silvery. But the thing I
noticed more than anything was his hat which was like a
bishop's mitre and pointed... and I realised that the angel
was telling me that he was going to take my father...''

AS WE HAVE seen in the previous chapter, a vast number of angel experiences that were reported to me related in differing ways to death and dying. Some idea of the soul or spirit seems to have played an important part in helping many different societies to express their conviction that life does not end with physical death.[2]

An angel of death is of course not a purely Christian concept – such entities are found in all cultures – the 'yamdoot' (the Indian Hindu death angel) and the wailing banshee said to presage death in Celtic communities are both typical examples. The folklore image of the Grim Reaper could well derive from these dark angel sightings.

According to my respondents, experiences varied from seeing angels as part of a near-death experience (NDE) or out-of-body experience (OBE) to witnessing angels immediately prior to an impending death, or at the actual moment of death (whether the respondent was present in the room at the time or not). In other cases, the experience happened in years subsequent to the death itself.

As discussed throughout the previous chapters, angels have been seen in many differing forms. The visionary experience of seeing a traditional-style angel is a constant thread throughout this chapter, as it was in the last. Such angels have been recorded as standing beside the bed of the critically ill as if silently waiting.

As discussed in chapter seven, smelling a distinct scent at the time of someone's death, either while they were in the same room at the time of death or without actually being in their presence is extremely common. Other people reported having the experience sometime after their loved ones had died.

Some letters to me recounted seeing an angel with the 'ghost' of the deceased person – some even saw both at the precise time of death as if the angel was there to escort the person to the next plane. Other respondents, though, have simply reported seeing the deceased person – a sight that some would perhaps term a 'ghost', but which they have attributed to being their guardian angel. Some people simply told me that they felt 'aware' of being in the presence of the dead.

Grief and bereavement

In every culture great mystery surrounds the concept of death, so it is perhaps not surprising that angelic experiences seem to feature quite highly at such distressing times. One of the seemingly obvious explanations to explain away the experience of seeing angels at the time of a death would be that such a vision is brought about by grief or bereavement. I have looked in depth at the whole area of death studies, but am convinced such an explanation is not sufficient. For example, Ramsey and de Groot[3] describe nine components of grief, some of which tend to appear earlier in the grief process, some of which come later. Although some of these components of grief could be used in analysis of after-death communication, or ADCs (explored later in this chapter) or visions (be they visions of an angel, a loved one or both) occurring *after* a loved one's death – none can in any way account for experiences happening at the actual moment of death – or in some cases, preceding the death, moments before the death was known about, so to have even entered any grieving stage would be impossible. Out of the nine stages, I think only Ramsey and de Groot's stage three (Denial) could be connected to the experiences disclosed in this research and even then could only account for an almost negligible number of the accounts received. We must remember that five-sixths of the experiences relate to spontaneous happenings before the person actually died. In today's society we are quick to find rational, logical explanations for mysteries, but as hard as I have tried, there are seemingly some that have no solid explanation.

After-death communication (ADC)

In order to talk about experiences around death we must first look briefly at after-death communication – experiences in which deceased relatives come back to impart messages to those they left behind. This is a phenomenon probably as old as mankind, with related stories being documented throughout all cultures – some spoken far more freely, without the taboos applied to them here in the UK. As with angel visions, not all grieving people have an ADC; the reason for this is unknown.[4]

In his 1958 study *Widows and their Families*, P. Marris[5] interviewed widows and found that many spoke of feeling that their husbands were still present; about half of the sample of bereaved people needing psychiatric treatment whom C.M. Parkes studied for his report *Bereavement and Mental Illness*[6] felt the same. Similarly, Rees[7] reported that one in eight widows and widowers had hallucinations that consisted of hearing their dead spouse speak, and a similar proportion claimed to have seen the deceased. They also referred to a general sensation of the dead person being present, which could continue for years, and they found it helped them; significantly, those who had been happily married reported this more often.

Like angel experiences, ADCs can appear in different forms and in many situations, such as smelling a fragrance, hearing a voice, seeing a vision or 'someone/something' preventing the recipient from having a potentially fatal accident. ADCs and angelic visions therefore share many commonalties and one really cannot be discussed without mention of the other.

Angel visions prior to death

Angel visions/experiences around death tend to happen either before or at the moment of death – only a minority of cases have been sent to me describing an experience happening afterwards. Given this fact, Mark Chorvinsky's research on Grim Reaper sightings[8] perhaps offers a more appropriate comparison than ADCs in this area of research. Chorvinsky has noted several cases in which dying people were seen to interact with an invisible, personified 'death', others in which witnesses close to death have met the Reaper (either driving it away or talking it out of taking them, thus surviving), or doctors or nurses who have witnessed the Reaper waiting beside the dying. Replacing the vision of the Reaper with that of an angel, my own data complements his findings. It's important to note the similarities and the differences between these two studies: with its dark clothes and scythe, the Grim Reaper is an instantly recognisable figure, whereas according to the range of experiences reported by my respondents, the appearance of an angel varies considerably, from merely a fragrance or the intangible bearer of a message, to a full-blown figure with wings or pure light. Whereas a Grim Reaper vision is seen as a negative experience, the after-effect of an angelic encounter around death is seen as being far more positive. Could we go so far as to say that today angel sightings around the time of death are outweighing Grim Reaper sightings? If this were the case it would provide a whole new angle on narrative and the use of vocabulary and the merging of ideas, representing a large step in death discourse as well as a shift in language, terminology and explanation of the dying process.

Otherworldly experiences at the time of death occur in many situations. Starting off with near-death and out-of-body experiences, we shall then look at angels in waiting – experiences in which angels are seen at the bedside of the terminally sick and dying. The phenomenon of scent in the presence of the dying is explored more fully in the previous chapter but is alluded to here. Thereafter, we will explore the subject of angels being present at the moment of death, both from respondents who were in their presence at the time and from those who were not. Finally we will look at the subject of angels seen after death and the fact that some people are convinced that a deceased relative has become their guardian angel.

Near-death experiences

With the advancement of modern medicine, people are being pulled back from death every day – however, it has been estimated that a staggering 40% of them are claiming to have experienced another dimension of reality that, they claim, exists beyond death. Great debate surrounds this concept, something that I want to discuss here, as there is already an abundance of literature around surrounding this idea. However, whether it may be explained physiologically, for example as a result of oxygen starvation to the brain, chemical activity in the brain (perhaps involving endorphins), or as a result of something else (it is claimed that the anaesthetic drug gives a perception of consciousness apart from the body, bringing about visions of a light and even feelings of love), it is important to remember that there is ongoing controversy regarding the degree of similarity between these experiences and NDE experiences. Whatever the stimuli, one thing that is certain is such experiences happen and have a great effect on the person they happen to.

Near-death experiences may occur during surgery, cardiac arrest, anaphylactic shock, coma, fever, anaesthetic, unconsciousness, accidents, physical injury, arrhythmia, seizures, suicide, severe allergic reactions and other physical trauma to the physical body. During such extreme states, the individual near death may feel themselves to be existing outside of their physical body. Their experience might include all or some of the following elements: going down a tunnel; seeing and or entering a light; meeting a deceased relative or heavenly being; coming to a precipice or place where a decision about life or death must take place; seeing their life pass before their eyes, sometimes in chronological order, when it is known as a 'life review'; acute awareness; a feeling of timelessness; and intense emotions.[9]

As in the experience of seeing angels, one could argue that the near-death experience is culturally determined – Muslims often report seeing Mohammed, Christians see Jesus and so forth. Of course, with angels (or entities of a comparable nature and role) being apparent in all religions, is not surprising that they crop up randomly in accounts. It is interesting to note that in all but one of the NDEs I have received, angels are seen in the traditional form – a person in white, sometimes with wings and surrounded by light.

One lady wrote, 'I was being operated on in hospital. I was very ill and started to float and was with beautiful angels and birds flying. I then was going through a tunnel. I went halfway then it all lit up and I saw no more. I will never forget it.'

Another of my female respondents has been diagnosed with a potentially fatal cancer and underwent major surgery:

Upon being wheeled back to my room I experienced the most amazing vision. I was travelling through a 'breathing' passage and found myself looking up into the most beautiful and magnificent domed area. It was guilded in bright, shining gold, and shone in the most amazing light. Smiling, joyful 'faces' floated past me, all gazing at me as they passed, bathing me in their goodness... Eventually I was again travelling down the breathing passage towards a light. I never reached it, but gradually awoke. I felt I had been shown a part of heaven.

Robin Wheeler wrote to me about an angelic encounter that his mother had in 1995:

At that time she was terminally ill with cancer of the throat and liver failure, and was in the Christie Hospital in Manchester. She had been in a coma for a week. On the Saturday morning, December 23, I got a call from the hospital saying we had better come in. Obviously this meant that she was dying, as far as the staff were concerned. I picked my sister up and drove in to the hospital When we got to her room, she was sitting up in bed, being washed by the nurses.

My sister... asked her how she had slept. She said, 'Fine, until that angel woke me up, sitting on my feet.' We, of course, both went 'Angel?', and I asked what it had looked like – did it have wings? Now although this seems like a terrible 'prompt', she was quite adamant that it did, saying. 'Of course! They came right down to the ground', and indicated wing tips with her hands. My sister asked her what it was wearing, and she said it was wearing a white robe. She went on, 'It had lovely inner... inner....' I asked 'innocence'? She said (again very emphatically) 'Yes.' One of us asked what it looked like, and she said, 'It had a dark face, you know, dark skin.' I asked 'Like a West Indian?' and she replied rather impatiently, 'No, just dark.'

... When we spoke to the nursing staff about why they had felt it necessary to call us in when she seemed to be relatively stable, they apologised, and said that at the time they had called us in she had no pulse, and was not breathing – as they put it, 'She had gone.' This would of course have been exactly the time she saw the angel.

The sequel to this, which shows that my mother clearly appreciated the significance of the angel's appearance (and that it was not wishful thinking on her part) was on Christmas day, when we went in to visit her again. I asked her if she remembered seeing an angel, and she said, 'Yes I do, and I don't want to see that again, because I know what that means.' This, by the way, was in marked contrast to the way she spoke about the appearance the first time, which was without any suggestion of fear or misgiving, but more with an air of wonder and admiration.

Unsurprisingly, the experiences recounted this chapter connect closely with those hospital experiences discussed in chapter eight. They also recall the account in chapter three in which Lloyd Glen's son, Brian, who was trapped beneath a garage door, underwent a near-death experience in which he was taken up into the sky with the 'birdies'.

Out-of-body experiences

In an out-of-body experience (OBE), the individual finds him- or herself out of their body, but their physical body is in absolutely no danger, nor in any danger of dying. Anyone can have an OBE – no special belief or ability is necessary. Some people have reported OBEs that have occurred while jogging, sleeping, praying, meditating or while piloting fighter aircraft.

Others report them while reading and while day-dreaming; however, they seem to occur most frequently during sleep.[9]

Tom's experience, which occurred when he was sixteen, is a perfect example. His father became seriously ill and, facing death, he found it easiest to talk about what there may be as an afterlife. Tom was interested in the subject of the afterlife himself and he and his father would often joke that when he died, and if there was something there, then he'd come back and tell Tom. A few months later his father died.

About six months after the death, while staying over one night with a group of lads at his friend's house, Tom experienced an OBE. He felt himself lift out of his body until he was looking down on himself. Panicking, he shouted down to his friends, who were all asleep on the floor, but they were all asleep and couldn't hear him. The main thing that concerned Tom was what would happen in the morning, when the others woke up to find him dead. His body would be carried away and burnt, leaving him all alone hovering above it! He continues:

> After the initial panic, I felt a presence by my side, guiding me along a long tunnel until I came to a fork and had to decide which way to go – I looked to my right and saw a huge and very beautiful staircase ascending upwards. On it, stood at every six or so steps, were pairs of angels, dressed in long white gowns, with wings clasped behind them. I really believe had I have gone up the staircase I would have been in 'heaven', with my dad, but I felt there was so much more to do on earth, that I wasn't ready to go there yet. Suddenly, with a jerk I landed back inside my body. I awoke and burst into tears, waking my other friends up, [and explained] hysterically what I'd just gone through.

To this day, Tom doesn't know what caused him to have this experience – his life was in no danger, nor had he had any alcohol or drugs. His only explanation is that his late father had kept his word, by showing him that indeed there was an afterlife.

Angels seen at the moment of death

This next category contains accounts that happened at the exact moment of death, with respondents falling into two groups. The first consists of those who had an experience at the very same time, but were not in their presence at the time – they were perhaps on the other side of the world or in the car on the way to the hospital, not realising the person they were coming to visit had passed away. The second group comprises those who were in the same room as the dying and had an experience the moment they took their last breath.

Respondent not in the presence of the dying

Raymond Wheeler wrote to tell me of an incident that happened some years ago:

> My grandmother (Mum's mum!) and her younger sister were in Eastbourne to visit my great-grandmother who was very ill and not expected to live very long. Walking away from the house one afternoon – and having found her very much at peace, though quite obviously very poorly – they were discussing the situation and, no doubt, preparing for the inevitable, when they were both stopped in their tracks and caught hold of one another, saying 'did you see that?' They both – independently – claimed to have seen two shining winged people, who [they] were convinced must have been angels, gently

escorting a human away. It was over in a second, but my grandma and aunty never forgot this experience, as they heard on their return home that their mum had died – at the precise moment they saw the angels; both were convinced that they had seen their mum's soul being escorted to the next life. Apparently the incident was only spoken about rarely in the months which followed, as the two were laughed at, particularly by some male in-laws, but my mum never doubted the existence of her mother's and aunt's experience...

As discussed in the chapter seven, many people reported that experiences around the time of death involved a scent. On the day Rosalie Double's mother died in 1952, Rosalie experienced an 'intense scent of fresh flowers – all separate and identifiable'; a similar experience occurred after the death of her husband, when the grandfather clock stopped at 2.25 – 'the exact time he himself died'.

Experiences involving clocks do not seem uncommon. Lynda Barton's father died Sunday evening at 9:30 p.m.:

... next morning the family realised all the clocks in the house had stopped at 9:30 p.m. We put this down to coincidence. Strangely enough, the following Sunday the clocks stopped again at 9:30 p.m. Shortly afterwards, I walked from the hallway to the lounge. As I put my hand on the light switch, a hand, 'unseen', pressed my hand against the switch enough to leave an impression in my palm. Initial fear [was] followed [by] a great sense of calm; as I walked into the lounge I sensed a feeling of 'wings' enfolding me. In the corner was a shape. Not identifiable as one would recognise as the Christmas card angel, but the same calm white figure that I had seen before.

Respondent in the presence of the dying

Based on the reports I have received, visionary angelic experiences seen at the moment of death always tend to feature the robed, winged type of angel dressed in white – not the description of the traditional 'angel of death'. This is a point worthwhile noting when we look at the cultural determination of experiences and the subject of whether people see what they want or expect to see.

The following experience occurred on December 1 1991 – the day Heather Erridge's father died peacefully from cancer:

> A very tall, glowing figure was next to his bed all the afternoon and evening of the Sunday he lay dying… as I held his hand, I became aware of a ten-foot presence kneeling on the opposite side of the bed, looking intently into my dad's face. The figure was tall, dressed in brilliant white, flowing robes, and glowing with a sparkling force which was eminently powerful… we both sat and watched my dad… Mum suddenly kissed him and asked me to 'come and say goodbye to your father'. A minute or so after this he died; Mum was one side of the bed, Tim [Heather's husband] and I the other. Mum promptly said I ought to pray or something – I was stunned because I had just watched my father slide feet first out of the foot end of the bed through the bedclothes, and go to join the glowing figure who was by now… [lighting the dull] corner of the room… he sat with the figure for a few minutes looking back on us all around the bed, and suddenly they were gone – the corner became dark again.

Suzanne's experience happened the night her grandmother died:

> Sitting with Gran as she lapsed between consciousness and unconsciousness we both knew that she was going to pass on, as she had been ill for a long while. I was no doubt afraid of what was going to happen as I had not experienced actually being with someone while they died. As I held her hand wanting her to know that I was with her, for what must have been many hours... I experienced someone sitting outside the window, her late husband, who had died when I was six years old, I was very close to him, he was a gentle person and was missed terribly by all the family (that was forty-one years ago).
>
> He spoke to me very gently, telling me that he had been waiting for Gran to join him for their journey, but was waiting for me to let her go, telling me not to rush as he had waited all those years.
>
> I became aware of someone sitting next to me, all was calm. I held Gran with my left hand and was aware of Frank holding my right hand I felt a gently but powerful rush of energy and strength pass through me. When I became more aware of what was happening I watched them in the form of angels fly off into a completely calm night [...] I had this thought they hesitated, until I thought, do not look back, fly away to your new adventure. Everything around me was totally calm, all I could do was look skyward into a clear night sky.

Another respondent told me of an 'incident... related to me some years ago by the aunt (now deceased) of the small boy involved. She was present on this occasion, and told me all about it as we returned from church one Feast of St Michael and All Angels...'

> Her elderly father lived with her married sister, husband and small son. One lunchtime, the boy (aged five or six) was told 'Go and tell Grandpa lunch will be ready in a few minutes.'
>
> This he did, but Grandfather did not come to the meal. After several more minutes, he was asked if he had told Grandpa the meal was ready.
>
> 'Yes,' came the reply, 'But Grandpa was busy.' Then – obviously as an afterthought – 'The room was full of angels.'
>
> They ran to Grandpa's room to find that he had died.

A similar experience happened in a large house with servant's bells, where the respondent's late aunt had an experience that happened the moment her father, a physically fit fifty-six year old, had suddenly and very unexpectedly died:

> A bell rang and my aunt saw that it indicated her father's bedroom – he had felt unwell and had gone to lie down. My aunt went to see what he wanted, but as she reached the stairs she was struck with awe and foreboding to see an angel in a bright shaft of light at the top of the staircase. When she got to her father's bedroom she found that he had just died.

Angel seen some time after death

Some sort of after-death communication is one of the most common spiritual experiences that people report. Research has shown that 50–75% of grieving spouses or parents have some sort of visitation after losing a loved one. However, most people trivialise or dismiss the experiences as grief-induced hallucinations, and cut themselves off from their potential to heal. There are three broad categories of healing spiritual visions surrounding death and dying: premonitions of death, shared dying experiences, and after-death visitations.

Relatively little systematic work has been done on postmortem visitations.[11] Dr M. Cleiren's study *Adaptation After Bereavement*[12] showed that 14 months after a death about one-third of the bereaved people studied felt a sense of presence of the dead and also 'talked' to the dead, either vocally or in a silent inner 'conversation'. Added to this, R.C. Finucane's *Appearances of the Dead: A Cultural History of Ghosts*, an historical analysis of the way in which the ghostly dead appear to the living, makes the point that up to the 18th century, ghosts were generally vocal while by the 20th century they tend to be mute.[13] This ties in with the reports of otherworldly experiences I have received – only one account depicted a deceased relative that actually spoke; however, in some accounts an angel accompanied the deceased, speaking on their behalf and making the assurance that all would be well.

Granny as your guardian

The very words people choose to describe their experience form a really interesting area of discussion, something my university work particularly focuses on. The largest hurdle I have come across is the tendency some respondents have to report the experience of seeing a deceased loved as their guardian angel, and not as a ghost or apparition. I have also received testimonies from people who report ADCs with deceased family members whom they believe now serve as 'angelic influences'. In such muddy waters, language can be confusing. There is the basic problem of what an angel is attributed to be. Ghosts, spirits, guides, angels, energies – all theoretically separate entities with their own description and connotations – become merged into one when people attempt to define what an angel represented to them. Could we go so far as to say all these entities are perhaps the same thing – or represent the same experience –with simply a different label? I would argue that for the large majority they could well be.

I found a classic example of a loved one returning with a message in Dr Melvin Morse's internet study 'Death-related Visions and healing Grief'. Dr Morse is a paediatrician and neuroscientist who has spent fifty years studying NDEs in children. One of Morse's patients had a vivid dream that her son would be horribly injured in a car accident. No details were given that could have led to her preventing the accident. Indeed, she was ultimately the driver in the wreck, and the accident was her fault. She told Morse that, to her, the meaning of her dream was that her mother, who had given her the news in her dream, was her guardian angel and watched over her. 'Without that dream,' she explained, 'I could never have kept my family together, been a wife, and a mother to my other children, because I felt so guilty and depressed over what I did. Yet I always knew that even though it was my fault, somehow it was meant to be, and my mother would always be there for me.'[14]

This is where we develop a shift in language and meaning – cases in which people have reported seeing deceased loved ones and attributing them to be their guardian angel. Such experiences range from those by which a life may actually be saved, such as David Barber's encounter which follows, to those in which a 'ghost' appears with a message or a warning, as it did in the form of Sylvie's late sister (both described below). Other experiences simply document seeing a deceased loved one either dressed as an angel or otherwise communicating the fact to the witness that they have become their guardian angel.

On March 14 1981, David Barber had taken his son Andrew to the local lido in Droitwich. Being a non-swimmer, David stayed in the shallow waters, but as his confidence grew he moved further down the pool, until:

> I slipped and fell onto the floor of the pool, I was under for a minute or two and I realised I was going to die. Then I saw my grandmother floating towards me. She'd been dead for about sixteen years, and I remember she was wearing a silky gown that wafted in the water. As her hands went underneath me, my head started banging against the bottom of the baths. When I looked up I saw my son trying to pull me. I don't think there was any way he could have pulled me up on his own, but with my grandmother, my guardian angel, lifting me too, I was brought to the surface.

Ray Grindall believes his late grandfather returned as an angel the moment his grandmother died, when he was a teenager living at home:

> I was sixteen and living with my parents and widowed grandmother, my grandfather (George) had died a few years earlier. Anyway, my grandmother became critically ill and was being nursed by my mother in an upstairs bedroom. My mother would sit at the bedside of my grandmother with our pet dog, Blackie, a cocker spaniel, for company. I must stress that Blackie was absolutely fearless, be it of humans or other animals.
>
> On this particular evening, my father and I were

sitting downstairs in the lounge listening to the radio when we heard something rushing down the stairs, whining and howling. As we opened the [...] door, Blackie rushed in with all the hair standing up on his back [...] rushed under the table, whining and cowering, and was absolutely petrified. My father then called out to my mother who was still upstairs and she then related what had happened.

As she was sitting at the bedside, my grandmother came out of the coma she was in, lifted her head from the pillow and without any sign of illness gave a brilliant smile, looked up to the corner of the room and said, 'Hello George' and at that second passed away. At the same second, Blackie who was laid at my mother's feet, shot up and looked in the exact place where my grandmother had looked, and with absolute terror, and hair on end, whining, shot out of the room and flew down the stairs to my father and I.

I am convinced that both my grandmother and Blackie had seen an angel that had come down for my grandmother in the guise of my grandfather.

In common with Ray's account, quite a few letters documented the experience of seeing deceased relatives and sensing that they had not become guardian angels. Mrs Brown, however, saw her late mother in angelic apparel. 'When I was a child [aged] eight and a half years, my mother died very suddenly, aged thirty-four. I am now elderly. I vividly remember going to bed and my mother stood at the bottom of the bed, dressed as an angel in white with wings. I was a nervous child and felt frightened, I pulled the sheet over my head and when I pulled it back she had gone.'

About halfway through his daughter's wedding reception

Llewelyn Rhys suddenly felt very cold and had a strong feeling of needing to be on his own: 'I looked up at the north end of the marquee, and there, without any doubt, was the outline of my grandmother's face. She died in 1946, and clearly had been "allowed back" to see her great-granddaughter married. The whole episode was all over in about three seconds.' Llewelyn had another similar experience after the funeral of a Scottish uncle, on January 3 1971. His uncle and he had been very close and Llewelyn noted that the uncle had acted very much 'in loco parentis' towards him:

> To cut a long story short, I had a curious but strong urge to walk to a lake in his grounds after the funeral reception. It was a kind of 'pulling' feeling. Suddenly I swung around and heard my late uncle sternly say, 'Are you sure you want this to happen?' It was the voice of my late uncle when he was, say, about twenty years younger. But I did not see anything.

Many of the respondents who wrote to me told of experiences involving messages from beyond the grave. Sylvie explained:

> It was only recently I received my 'white feather' showing an angel was near... I was on holiday this summer in Bournemouth [...] I was alone in the lift going to my room. I stepped out at the third floor and as the door opened, there on the floor in front of me was a white feather, which I picked up and carry with me all the time. I think it was my sister, who had died a year before, and I was aiming to visit her grave the following week when her headstone was to be blessed. We were very close and since that I have seen her in my home and received several messages for her

daughter. [I] always get a certain smell (of potpourri) before she appears and all the messages have been accurate and meaningful.

Jack Hunter's late grandfather appeared to him with a message at a highly opportune time. After coming home on leave from the RAF in 1941, Jack decided to call on his GP before he returned to his wing. The doctor suggested he attend a chest clinic for an X-ray:

I was given a complete examination by the consultant. He then told me that I wasn't to concern myself about returning to the RAF as he would be contacting them to inform them that he was sending me to hospital – […] I had TB.

Over a year later, still in the City Hospital, Edinburgh I really started to get worse – I had developed pneumonia and other complications, so I was moved into a special small ward. It was during the smallpox epidemic here in Scotland, which started in Aberdeen, and no visitors were allowed into the hospital, as one of the wards was used for the smallpox patients. I was told years later that a policeman had been sent to my home to warn my father and mother I wasn't expected to survive.

But survive I did, and a few weeks later I was taken back into the big ward with the other thirty or so patients. I was X-rayed again for the consultant to cheek my progress when he made his weekly visit. He held [the X-ray] up to the window to compare it to one taken just a few weeks before then turned to the ward doctor and said, 'That's amazing, they don't look as if they were taken from the same patient.' Then, as he was going to walk on, [he] turned to me and said, 'Keep up the good work, that's good chap.' Was this my first experience of my guardian angel?

When I was eventually discharged from hospital after two and a half years, the staff nurse asked the Big White Chief for his prognosis, to which he replied he thought I could survive about twenty years providing I looked after myself, which would mean [he thought I would survive until] my middle forties.

After a few months at home my sister invited me to stay with her at Ancum in the Borders, as a sort of convalescence. Unfortunately I took ill again after another few months and her GP suggested a return to hospital – a sanatorium at Hawick. I was awaiting availability of a bed there when one night this vision appeared at the foot of the bed. I recognised him as my grandfather and he said that I wasn't to worry as he was looking after me! I remember being very surprised that it was my grandfather, as I had just been six when he died.

My stay in the sanatorium lasted nearly two years again and then I was sent to Bangour Hospital in West Lothian for a thoracoplasty operation. When I finally arrived home I was twenty-eight. I restarted work when I was thirty and retired at sixty-five. I am now seventy-eight; [I] have a wife who has taken great care of me [and] have two grown up children and four grandchildren.

ANGELS IN THE NIGHT: ENTERING THE TWILIGHT ZONE

'Very suddenly an angel appeared…
I do not remember a face — just two absolutely
massive wings… I remarked how large, how
beautiful these wings were. It seemed the wings were
of the greatest importance.'

THERE IS A brief time while we lie in bed at night, neither fully awake nor yet asleep, when we pass through a twilight mental zone. Many people associate this drowsy stage with hallucinatory images, more fleeting and disjointed than dreams, and compare it to watching a speeded-up, jerky series of photographic slides. A host of artists and scientists have credited the imagery of this twilight state with creative solutions and inspiration for their work.[1] Like many others, I can certainly relate to this – we all seemingly have the best of ideas and find answers to problems when we are most relaxed, just on the edge of sleep or upon waking in the night. Your body feels half-asleep but for some reason your brain is in overdrive.

We are now beginning to understand that during this brief somnolent state, people not only have creative insights but

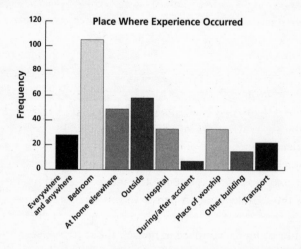

may also be more in touch with the unconscious in general. There is even evidence that the suspension of critical judgment associated with the usually dominant left hemisphere of the brain may allow the non-dominant right side of the brain, with its more intuitive and emotional processes, to take over.[2]

As the table above indicates, the vast number of respondents to this study – 30% in fact – recounted experiences that had occurred in the bedroom, with 9.5% happening around a hospital bed (as explored in chapter eight). All of these visions have been reported to occur just as they are falling to sleep, in the early hours of the morning or upon waking. This half-awake, half-asleep level of awareness is usually referred to as the twilight state or the alpha state. From here on I shall term these experiences 'twilight experiences'. According to my data, they appear to be a very common occurrence.

The narratives of many of the letters I received contained strikingly similar passages. For example: 'I certainly did not dream it, but I can't explain exactly what it was I saw, other than an angel'; 'I know I wasn't dreaming it, as I was very much aware of what was happening.'

The Twilight State: beta, alpha, theta and delta

The theta state is a state of mind often referred to as the 'twilight' state, that which precedes delta, or deep sleep. While in the theta state, the mind can recall vivid memories, have sudden insights, creative inspiration, high productivity, feelings of serenity, and 'oneness' with the universe... It is in this state that one can fully experience the imagery and thoughts that pass through the mind. A person in this state passes gently and freely from consciousness to sub-consciousness. Alfred Einstein could intentionally induce in himself the theta brainwave state, and often did so when seeking creative insights in his work.

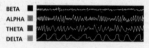

BETA	Alertness, concentration; focus and cognition
ALPHA	Relaxation, visualisation and creativity
THETA	Intuition, memory, meditation and vivid visual imagery
DELTA	Deep sleep, healing and detached awareness[1]

EEG equipment distinguishes these waves by measuring the speed with which neurons fire in cycles per second:

BETA WAVES range between 13–40 HZ. The beta state is associated with peak concentration, heightened alertness and visual acuity. Nobel Prize winner Sir Francis Crick and other scientists believe that the 40 HZ beta frequency used on many brain sync tapes may be key to the act of cognition.

ALPHA WAVES range between 7–12 HZ. This is a state of deep relaxation, but not quite meditation. In alpha, we begin to access the wealth of creativity that lies just below our conscious awareness – it is the gateway, the entry point that leads into deeper states of consciousness. Alpha is also the home of the window frequency known as the Schuman Resonance, which is the resonant frequency of the Earth's electromagnetic field.

THETA WAVES range between 4–7 HZ. Theta is one of the more elusive and extraordinary realms we can explore. It is also known as the twilight state, which we normally only experience fleetingly as we rise up out of the depths of delta upon waking, or drifting off to sleep. In theta we are in a waking dream, vivid imagery flashes before the mind's eye and we are receptive to information beyond our normal conscious awareness. Theta has also been identified as the gateway to learning and memory. Theta meditation increases creativity, enhances learning, reduces stress and awakens intuition and other extrasensory perception skills.

DELTA WAVES range between 0–4 HZ. Delta is associated with deep sleep. In addition, certain frequencies in the delta range trigger the release of Growth Hormone beneficial for healing and regeneration. This is why sleep – deep, restorative sleep – is so essential to the healing process.[3]

There are many ways in which one can enter the twilight state – for example through meditation, relaxation techniques, hypnosis, and deep prayer. However, this state of awareness can also be entered spontaneously through daydreaming or from simply feeling creative.[4] According to the data I have collected, it certainly seems that the majority of angelic experiences occur when people are either very relaxed or, at the other end of the scale, when facing imminent danger. The two different states which I believe are of interest to this work are the alpha and theta waves. It is during both these states that angelic experiences are most apparent.

More than a dream

> *'Six weeks after his death my father appeared to me in a dream... it was an unforgettable experience, and it forced me for the first time to think about life after death.'* CARL JUNG

We all have dreams – sometimes we remember them, more often we don't; equally, some dreams are more meaningful and vivid than others. The following accounts are taken from what a respondent to this study interpreted as a dream – but for one reason or another, it was more than a dream.

To be honest, after looking into the alpha state and twilight experiences it has surprised me how few people reported seeing angels in their dreams and counted them as true experiences. Many cases of angelic visitations have been reported in the case of after-death communication and I thought this trend would follow through in my research but it has not.

Mrs Graham was eighteen and very ill with glandular fever although she was not on any medication. As she cat-napped, she saw '... a Mediterranean blue background with four of five of these figures – white "cartoon nuns" as I called them at the time (I had attended a convent until seventeen...) – they were still, and one or two of them "flitted" occasionally. This seemingly lasted for seconds. When I awoke I knew everything was going to be fine and though I was at my worst... I felt very "still" and "good" about everything.'

The other angelic experiences that came in the form of dreams tended to be predicatory in nature – especially foretelling the unexpected deaths of loved ones. In December 14 1983, Alan was in Canada where he had lived since emigrating in 1973. He awoke after a vivid dream involving his father with an angel: 'It was really a soft light with a soft, blank face. Well, Dad had this halo around his head and seemed to be floating in this light, that's all I remember of the dream/vision.' Two days later Alan's father unexpectedly died, and when he arrived back in England and saw the expression on his father's face in the morgue chapel it brought back the vision – it was the identical expression that his father had worn in the dream.

Mrs Ellis also had a dream that seemed to pre-empt a death:

> I dreamed I and my husband were walking in mountains and came to a stand side by side overlooking the most beautiful valley. We were so very happy. Then from behind and from the left there glided a lovely lady in a very white long dress, all silky with folds to the ground. She came up behind us and put her hand on my husband's shoulder and together they glided back and to the left where she had come. (I didn't look round but in my dream still looking over the valley I could see all about me). I felt a tremendous sense of loss and awoke upset. My husband comforted me and said 'It's only a dream'. I remember I kept repeating 'But she took you away –

she took you away' and I couldn't stop crying. Within
a short while my husband died. I felt the dream had
been telling me this.

The following two dream accounts are connected to angelic
experiences that happened at the precise moment of death
though the person was not in the presence of the dying, as
seen in the previous chapter. Thomas is an Indian national
working as a senior camp boss for a large company out in the
Republic of Yemen. He writes:

My father died in the year 1986 after a long illness.
[At] that time I was working in Doha Qatar. He
breathed his last at exactly 3 o'clock a.m. It was
Wednesday. I had a dream in the night. A cute boy
with wings appeared me in the dream and told me
[that] something unexpected [was] going to happen.
He just turn his face and flew away. His face was just
shining like anything. Suddenly I got up – and looked
around… I [switched] on the light; it was ten minutes
to three. I couldn't sleep again. I could feel something
had happened to someone close to me. I started
thinking about my parents and relatives. With a heavy
heart I went to work. There was a telephone call from
one of my friends saying that my father had died at 3
o'clock. Everything flashed through my mind
including the dream I had. I still cannot give an
explanation of the dream I had and the subsequent
information of the death.

Ron Wells writes of the death of his wife:

Meg was quite clearly dying. She was paralysed

except for a little movement in her left hand, and the muscles of her face. She was deaf, blind and dumb. She communicated with us who came to give our love by gently squeezing two of our fingers placed in her left hand... But could she tell who was who? I had somehow to tell her that it was me, her lover and husband of nearly sixty years. Instead of a kiss I would sometimes caress the beautiful skin just below her throat; a very private and secret way of saying I love you. I did it, the corners of her mouth lifted in a sweet smile – she knew who it was [...] I came away from the hospital anxious and worried.

I managed eventually to get to sleep that night, but it was a restless, troubled sleep. Then, quite suddenly, I was wide awake. I looked at the bedside clock. It was four o'clock in the morning. Strangely, all my worry seemed to have vanished. I was relaxed, calm and peaceful. It was a wonderful peace, such as I could never remember having experienced before. I basked in it, free from all anxiety. All was well. I drifted into a deep, dreamless sleep... I was awakened at a quarter to seven by the telephone ringing. 'We very much regret... Mrs Wells... died peacefully and without pain... at four o'clock this morning.'

There had been prayers at Christ Church for her the day before, and my own feeble efforts in the evening. Who had sent me that wonderful message? All was well. Was it Meg herself? A dying woman whose brain was at last destroyed? Telepathy, you might say... I assent, without any doubt, that a miracle was performed. No known law of nature will account for the reality of that message. God had suspended his own laws for the love of a dear, precious, redeemed soul who had perhaps asked Him, 'Please tell Ron that all is well'...[5]

An angel at my bedside

It could be said that one of the rooms where we are at our most relaxed state is our own bedroom – that, combined with the fact we spend such a percentage of our time in that room, are surely contributing factors to the fact that such a high percentage of experiences are reported as taking place there.

Some respondents reported watching the bedclothes metamorphose into angelic wings, or, in Maureen Henry's words, 'angelic wings covering my bed as a bedspread... I am aware of being totally enveloped by their presence...', a phenomenon that she maintains has happened countless times over a few decades. Others simply see a traditional-style angel upon waking in the night, or, like Eleanor Fisher, while reading: 'I turned to put my book away and switch out the lamp. However, as I went to lie down I felt a bright light radiating from the corner of the room; glancing over I saw a beautiful young girl, clothed in blue, silver and white looking back at me and smiling.' Eleanor felt totally at ease, instantly realising she was looking back at an angel – a very pretty, fair-skinned woman whose head was basked in light and stood just two foot away from her! Transfixed by the experience, Eleanor stared back at the angel for several minutes, watching her slowly fade away, 'with her face (and smile) being the last thing to finally melt'. At this she sat bolt upright in bed, to see and smell a vast array of beautiful flowers that were scattered all over her bookcase. Immediately Eleanor leapt out of bed to turn the main light on to get a clearer view – as she did this, all the flowers and the scent disappeared.

About 10 years ago, Doreen Lloyd 'awoke and saw a figure of a young man aged about twenty-four, dark haired, with a stubbly short beard, dressed in a chenille striped yellow, red and green dressing gown-style garment. I took him to be an Arab, he communicated with me mentally, then went away via our son's bedroom. He did not frighten me, but I obeyed his mental advice. Another night I awoke to see a Zulu warrior-style figure, with three white stripes painted across his cheeks in an upward direction, though he may have been a Maori. He also communicated with me mentally that I had forgotten about our "triangle" for meditation. I was glad of this reminder, as I had clean forgot.'

Janet Newton's angel 'was enormous and looked like an angel with long flowing robes and wings [...] He was standing behind me, as I was lying in bed between sleep and wakefulness. I have been quite ill with cancer and was in the middle of chemotherapy treatment [at the time] and at a low state of mind. I'm not religious in the conventional way – but have a lot of friends praying for me and thinking of me. My angel bent down and kissed me – just above my mouth. The feeling was so profound I asked my husband if he had given me a kiss, but he denied this.'

Joanne Hird had unbearably painful sciatica – 'The births of my children were not as painful and of shorter duration – I saw two angels hovering in the bedroom. They looked exactly like pictures you see of angels on greeting cards. They had blond hair and were dressed in blue and gold robes. They said that if I got out of bed and just gave a little jump I would rise up and they would catch hold of me and I would be in no more pain but would not see my family again. They were in no hurry and asked if that was what I really wanted.

'Of course, it wasn't and they disappeared. I put it down to the brain playing tricks or a sort of hallucination. However, having said that I think I believe that there are different kinds of life ranging from minerals and plants through to animals, humans and up to God (of whatever religion). Angels would be a category between humans and God.'

Tracey-Anne O'Mara writes that she was 'either sleeping or meditating, I can't remember which, and I opened my eyes to see sitting several feet away an angel. It was the size of a ten-year-old child. It was coppery in colour, with wings, and was sitting upright on the floor with its knees bent in front of [it] and his hands resting on them. It was just sitting there looking at me. It had the presence of a gentle child and was very calming – it disappeared after a few seconds.'

Joy Prangley and her husband were relaxing in their lounge one Sunday afternoon. Joy closed her eyes in the hope of drifting off, but was unable to…

> … very suddenly an 'angel' appeared. The figure itself did not seem to have importance – I do not remember a face – just two absolutely massive wings – quite extraordinary. As I visualized this I was relating what I was seeing to my husband. I remarked how large, how beautiful these wings were. It seemed the wings were of the greatest importance. Very suddenly (just as the 'angel' had come) it disappeared. I was left feeling peaceful and more content that all would be well…

Just as the above respondents described seeing traditional-style angels, the following recounted seeing either a figure in white or someone they didn't recognize. Paul woke some months ago to find 'unless my eyes deceived me – a young woman standing beside my bed. She just faded away before my eyes. What I saw, or why she was there I just don't know.'

Mrs McSweeney saw '… a nun standing by my bed, stroking the covers. I was very afraid. I had lost my mother, and a friend introduced me to a medium. Much to my surprise, the nun spoke to me and apologised for startling me, but she explained she was my guardian angel and was there to protect me, which I know is so true, with [respect to] certain happenings in my life.'

Janet writes of how she experienced a visit from an angel in 1997.

> For some time I had felt deep personal pain, nothing like I had felt before, not even when my father died. In public I hid it to a certain extent, but in private (I live alone) it was very difficult to put aside.
>
> It was shortly after Princess Diana died that I woke to see the face of a woman, middle aged with blonde hair cut around the shape of her face. Her head was engulfed in light. As we looked at each other, she smiled and slowly faded away. My cat was asleep beside me and she did not flinch an inch. The peace I felt I had never felt before. I wasn't scared or frightened by it, but it took some time before I could get back to sleep. I was hoping she'd appear again.
>
> It wasn't until the following morning that I really thought anything about it. All my life I have lived in old properties, even now, where people have lived and died, and have never experienced any kind of presence… since then I feel a more happier and level-headed person, more relaxed about things. To this day I have never seen her since. I don't feel anything in particular, but I felt she was letting me know that everything was going to be OK.

June was looking out of her bedroom window one night when she was sixteen and saw '… a full moon with a beautiful lady at the back of it, throned in light and holding a child in her arms – an angel without wings.'

Richard Malone's experience happened whilst he was working as a managing director in New York back in 1991:

> At that time I was thirty-eight years old and was living on my own in an apartment... I suppose I was under considerable stress, typical of my Wall Street job. Anyway, one night I woke abruptly out of sleep to see a human figure, arrayed in classic splendour at the foot of my bed, shining, or rather scintillating, in a rippling golden light, with arms outstretched. An intense physical sensation spread very slowly throughout my body, to the tips of my fingers and toes, in a form completely unknown to me. It was an ecstatic and solidly physical experience. I recall being alarmed, I felt I was conscious... It was not sexual (indeed it was many times more intense), and then the sensation recurred and gradually faded away along with the apparition. It left a profound impression on me, and has not recurred. I have never taken psychoactive drugs, had not been drinking, and have no other explanations for the experience. I am solidly agnostic.

An answer to our prayers

In the 1980s, Vanessa Lillingston-Price was spending some time living with her parents; her room was at the top of the old house. On many occasions she reported to have felt negative or evil feelings on that particular floor and particularly hated going to sleep at night; she would pray for God's presence to protect and reassure her. One night, after praying she was wrapped in a cocoon of light that she knew nothing could break through, and experienced the most restful sleep in a long time!

The following night she prayed for a similar experience but the room and area around her bed remained dark. She waited for a while and then gradually became aware of the presence of a huge being sat on the bed. She continues:

> It wasn't something I was seeing with my eyes, but I was seeing it (if you can understand that!). He – for he seemed more male that female – appeared warrior-like, with a vast stature and broad chest and limbs. Although I couldn't guess his exact height, his presence seemed to fill the whole room to the extent that nothing else could possibly get through the door unless the angel decreed [it]. He was dressed in armour – like that of a Roman centurion – and his strength I imagine would have made Samson appear child-like!... I was in awe of him and felt that he must have had to leave some vast spiritual battle just to keep me company. I remember being very apologetic and saying how sorry I was that someone like him had to stop whatever he was doing to come and babysit for me – for babysitting is what it seemed by comparison... It wasn't as if we exchanged words per se, but I knew he could understand the thoughts I addressed towards him. I did not wait for a reply. I wouldn't have wanted him to speak to me, such was the degree of awe (fear!) I felt! Instead I turned over and went swiftly off to sleep.

Vanessa wasn't the only person who wrote saying that prayers had been answered. Some fifty years ago, Katherine Cook also saw an angel dressed in warrior-like armour:

> I could never bring myself to talk about it to anyone, even my mother. I was so overawed at the experience. It was that time, about 1950, [when] polio was a very serious complaint, before jabs [and the like were]

available. I had my five-year-old son in bed and very ill, the doctor called to visit him and told me that he couldn't say which complaint was developing, but he would have a better idea in twenty-four-hours' time and call around the next day to find out what had happened overnight. I was very upset and, being a Roman Catholic, I was on my knees praying most of the night and day that my son might be a bit better before the doctor called to examine him, when I saw the angel – huge, dressed in gold and white armour-type gear. I remember the helmet very well, gold and just like today's ice-hockey players wear in leather. My son recovered and the complaint was not polio, thankfully. I still cannot talk about this and am only writing because of the other lady telling in your article that she also saw this angel – I thought it might help another person in distress to take heart.

Jean Hess and her sister used to sleep in a brass bed complete with knobs, brass balls and a rail…

… as we were both nervous of the dark, we were allowed to have a night light – a small candle standing in a saucer of water, by our bed. It was on a small table to the right of us. Even so, we didn't like the flickering shadows thrown on the wall by the laundry bag and ornaments on the shelf, so we comforted ourselves by singing the following hymn:

> 'Lord keep me safe this night
> Secure from all my fears
> May angels guard me while I sleep
> Till morning light appears.'

After I had sung this one night, something seemed
to tell me to turn my head. Sitting on the rail behind
us were the shadows of two girl angels – one with
long waving hair, one with shorter hair (we both had
short, bobbed hair). Their wings were spread
protectively over us. I immediately felt peaceful and
happy. 'They've come,' I told my sister. Neither of us
felt surprised. We had asked for angels, and we had
got angels, and we turned over and went to sleep
knowing we were safe. If large shining angels had
come we might have been awed and afraid.

Of course, when we told our mother about this
wonderful occurrence the next morning, she said we
must have been dreaming, but we could not both have
had the same dream, could we? My sister still
remembers that night although she is seventy-five and
I am just seventy-three now. I would like to say further
that the silhouettes of our angels were clear and
unwavering and furthermore that the only small light
in our room was to the right.

Back in 1953, Jean Kerr was living in Zanzibar in an old
African Arab-style house in the port area. Her husband was ill
and was in the local hospital leaving her alone in the house
with their toddler and small baby. She writes that there were
'no other Europeans living within half a mile and I felt very
nervous and responsible for my two young children. There
were Arab crews from the Dhows and they slept just outside
rolled up in mats. I used to pray really hard for comfort and
peace and then one night I became aware of a white form at
the end of the bed through the mosquito net. Instead of being
terrified I became aware of the most wonderful peace and aura
in the room, and *knew* that God had sent an angel or messenger

to guard us – not [just] that night but all the nights until my husband came home. [I] have never forgotten that wonderful feeling of peace and safety. [I] believe very sincerely and humbly in guardian angels.'

Mr Hedge's experience was rather different in the sense that both he and his brother recognised the angel – it was their father, still alive, but away at sea, so it certainly wasn't a ghostly apparition:

[It all] happened some fifty odd years ago during the last world war when I was a young boy aged about six or seven years old. My brother (two years older) and I always said our prayers. One particular prayer contained the line 'may angels guard us while we sleep'. One particular night we had been sent to bed with a good whacking from our mother for misbehaviour. We shared the same bedroom and were terribly upset and crying our eyes out for a considerable time. I cried and cried for my father! Suddenly the bedroom door opened and our father walked in and spoke to us and told us that everything was alright and not to cry but to go to sleep.

A complete feeling of calm filled the bedroom and we settled and went to sleep. The next day we got up and rushed into the living room to see Dad and asked Mum where he was. She thought we were daft, as father was away at sea in the Royal Navy. Although we only saw him on occasions when he came home on leave, both my brother and I saw him in our bedroom that night and nothing would persuade us otherwise. Certainly there were no other men in the house and we certainly recognised our dad.

This event is still vivid in my memory and I've

always thought it was a guardian angel that was sent to comfort us. There were no bright lights or flowing robes or such like, just an intense feeling of peace, calm and well being. An angel? What else!

A similar thing happened to Elizabeth Sadik's mother:

My mother – in her late seventies – lived her widowed life in a bungalow on the coast. She was quite alone [and] was a nominal C. of. E. My husband was abroad. Very late one night she rang me to say that she felt very unwell and was frightened. I talked to her as reassuringly as I could and told her to ring her doctor. I did not know what to do and there was no one near I could telephone. The thought came to me to hire a minicab (I do not drive); it would have been a journey of some two and a half hours. But I didn't. I felt quite helpless to help her and frightened too! I fell on my knees and prayed and prayed. Then I immersed myself in the strong techniques of visualisation which I had tried to learn in Eastern disciplines. I fell asleep. Early next morning my mother rang. She said she felt better. And, 'It was lovely to see you darling, but how did you get out of the house when the three doors are still bolted on the inside?' I was stunned. I was so full of gratitude. I stumbled into the Church adjacent to us to make my offering of thanks.

Visitations to a child's bedroom
As a young child, Mrs. Beadle vividly remembers awakening to see angel:

To this day I do not know the reason why I was able

to see the angel then, except perhaps to relate that I had seen one, when angels have cropped up in conversation, or even perhaps for your research.

I don't know what caused me to wake and open my eyes. It was a moonlit night, so the bedroom was not dark and I could see the angel standing next to my bed, facing towards the bed head. He was golden and glistened… His hands were clasped at about lower chest level and he just stood there while I looked at him. I stretched out my arm and my hand went through him. I ducked my head under the bedclothes, in case I was dreaming, but when I looked again he was still standing there, motionless. Although I was not afraid I covered myself with the bedclothes again and when I looked again he was gone. The experience probably lasted no longer than five minutes. I did not find it frightening in any way. I think this is due to being brought up to say my prayers at night and going to Sunday School at the village Methodist Chapel, where Bible stories of the nativity, in which angels play their part, were taught…

Diving under the covers as a child seemed to be a regular theme among my respondents! In late 1939 or early 1940, when Malcolm Lewendon was seven or eight he was in bed with his mother, brother and sister – the family had only one bedroom – during wartime. He writes:

My sister Ann was about ten months old and was ill with pleurisy and pneumonia. I awoke one night and at the bottom of the bed stood an angel with arms outstretched and dressed in white. I yelled at my mother and said there's an angel at the bottom of the bed. She said to go to sleep. I put my head under the bedclothes – I was scared. I then peeped out and it was still there and then it just went. My sister recovered and is still well, so maybe the angel was there for some purpose.

Patricia Potter's mother went to bed one night while her boyfriend was away at war...

When she was a young girl in the First World War she worked the boats in Newport docks. She was in the habit of going to bed early – reading and eating chocolate! One night she was doing just that when she looked at the recess in the corner of the room and there stood an angel looking at her – an adult angel – well, to put it mildly she was terrified and dived under the bedclothes.

When she told her mother (my gran) the next day she was told not to be so silly – that she imagined it. Well, the next night she was lying in bed when the angel came and stood at the foot of the bed looking at her. She was afraid to go the next night until the rest of the family went.

A few days later her mother was in bed reading the newspaper when she suddenly said, 'Oh my God – the *Black Prince* has been blown up in the Jutland Battle.' My mother's boyfriend was a young sailor on board the *Black Prince* and of course was killed. My mother wondered if the angel had come to warn her. She never altered her story and she never forgot it.

During the Second World War, Jim Giles and his mother

stayed overnight with a neighbour for company:

This was in the early days of the Blitz. A lad of around twelve years of age, I was just going off to sleep one night when I felt some sort of presence which I find hard to describe. The door of the room was open and I glanced out to the hallway, which was bathed in a faint glow. At this point I distinctly saw a very beautiful young woman, with a luminous halo over her head. She was holding a beacon or some sort of light. This lasted for about four to five seconds, then gradually dissolved along with the glow. I stayed awake for some time gathering my thoughts. The whole experience had a sort of calming effect. The next day I told my mother about this, following which she decided to go to a local spiritual meeting to relate my experience. She was told that my apparition, if one can call it that, was a wonderful thing to witness, and signified that my family and I would get through the war unscathed. Dad was a London fireman and had a few narrow escapes, but, sure enough, he, Mum and I got through the whole six years without a scratch. I am now sixty-nine years of age, and have always been convinced that what I saw was, indeed, a guardian angel; a lovely, unforgettable happening.

When Lynne Pratley was six years old she awoke in the middle of the night to find the bedroom 'filled with a white light which radiated from the figure standing in a corner. This all-white, androgynous being was ceiling-high, robed with folded wings...'

He was not looking directly at me but downwards, and his arms were outstretched. I remember it very clearly as if it were yesterday and just stared in wonder for the five or so minutes of the visitation. He was very beautiful, Rossetti's angel of 'Ecce Ancilla Domini' is brought to mind.

I don't know [why] he chose to visit me; I was not ill or in trouble at the time. It was not a frightening experience – just, well, wonderful. For two consecutive nights afterwards, in bed before I went to sleep, a single white flame appeared and hovered above the bed. That I did find rather disturbing. I have not had other sightings, so I suppose I must conclude that he was my guardian angel. I don't know, none of my family or friends have ever scoffed at my recollections, in any case.

Louise Lyndon recalls an experience from when she was three years old:

I remember it as clear as if it were yesterday. From what I can remember it was quite late at night and my parents were in bed. I remember waking up and seeing an 'angel'-type figure sat on my rocking chair, I kind of knew it was a man. He was dressed in a white toga-type dress, he had huge wings and a halo, he glowed a brilliant white colour and lit up the whole room, I didn't see his face at all and he was probably only there for about thirty seconds. He was holding a letter, and to this day I have no idea what that was. I wasn't scared but I remember knocking on the wall to my parents' room, and as soon as my mother opened the door the room went dark and the figure had gone. My mum actually does remember this night. She said as a three-year-old child at the time I said, 'There was a man with a light on his head.' And to this day I still recall every detail of that experience, which is quite shocking as I was only three at the time. I have never seen anything since [and] I'll always feel as if I'm protected. Even now, years later… I still wonder why an angel appeared to me that night and why was he holding a letter?'

Night light

Light has been a common thread throughout all the visions of angels, whether the apparition itself was bathed in light or a beam of light was interpreted as being an angel. Visions of light at nighttime were a common feature in the communications that I received – doubtless such an apparition is an even more potent experience when it takes place in a darkened room.

A young soldier wrote while he was serving in the forces, placed out in Germany. He described being in bed one night and was startled to see 'two balls of light appear and "hover"', over his bed, 'moving about in a figure-of-eight-style pattern; after a few minutes the light metamorphosed into an angel', which looked down on him, smiling before slowly disappearing. From this he realised he was not alone and ceased to be afraid.

Others reported simply seeing a light. Chris Hopkins writes:

My experience was around two to three years ago. I was going through a particular stressful time at work, occasionally waking up through the night with work issues turning over in my head […] I do keep a small New Testament in my bedside cabinet and I have been known to read on occasions at difficult times to search for comfort in the words.

Anyway, one evening as indicated above it was a stressful time and I prayed for help and invited God into my life [...] whilst lying in bed. Then an incredible light came into the bedroom [...] It was the sort of brightness that you could see through closed eyelids (I didn't open my eyes) it could have only lasted a matter of seconds. Afterwards I felt an incredible warmth and comforting, a lifting of a weight and I remember sleeping deep and peacefully for the rest of the night. I didn't feel it necessary to join a church or anything and don't feel any more religious; however, something happened that night!

Avril writes:

It's true that it's during crises that angels appear to people – well, it is certainly true of my experience. My life up to then was traumatic, a very unhappy abused child and an even more abused young wife with five lovely children whom I adored, I found it harder and harder to cope. I turned to alcohol for relief, energy, and an escape from my dreadful reality. I became addicted for ten years and was separated from my children, which I could not bear. This separation caused me to go to AA and I was set free from my addiction. I had one year's sobriety, completely free of alcohol and all other chemical mind-altering substances. I say this to stress that I was in my right mind when I witnessed my angels. I was still extremely stressed out with longing for my children though, and emotionally wrecked. One night after tossing and turning for hours, I fell into a troubled sleep, I don't recall how long I'd slept but I was suddenly awakened [in] a state of super alertness by a strange tingling in my foot. I sat up in one movement and there, at the foot of the bed were two beings of light. No facial features visible, just vaguely human-shaped and human-sized beings, one slightly larger than the other; they were human-shaped halos of light (perhaps 'auras' is a better words than 'halos'). I was transfixed with wonder and all thought was suspended in a moment of eternal pure being and I will never know how long my eyes gazed upon such an amazing sight as this. Then, just as a question mark was forming in my head, I heard, telepathically, the larger saying to the smaller 'She sees us' in a voice which told of 'mission accomplished'. The larger moved around the bed towards me and seemed to reach out and as 'he' moved closer I sank back into my pillows and slept till the middle of the next day. When I awakened I had a quiet joy and peace about me that I had never experienced before in all my very troubled life [...] I [...] had difficulty analysing these strange feelings. I also had a deep sense that all would be well, which turned out to be the case...

However, in an interesting aside, Avril added 'I have come across many psychological explanations for experiences of this nature, but none of them fit mine. For instance, previous to my encounter with the angels, if you had asked me to draw what an angel looked like I would have portrayed the stereotype winged male/female, with pietistic expression, otherworldly, with hands clasped in prayer and eyes cast up to heaven. The *last* thing I'd have described is what I witnessed.'

After John Williams's wife passed away in January 1996, he found great difficulty in sleeping and often lay awake. One particular night he began to notice on the ceiling 'what I can only describe as pools of white soft light...'

> I put it down to light from the street lamp outside
> until I realised that the lamp is amber; even when I
> made sure the curtains were drawn properly the lights
> would still be there, but not every night. I was still
> very sceptical until the night of Sunday 23 February
> 1997, when I had been asleep. I woke up and there
> directly above me was what I can only describe as a
> shimmering white oval light of intense energy. How
> long it lasted I couldn't tell you. But since then the
> pools of light stopped appearing and only visit
> occasionally. The pattern of the lights as they
> appeared were as follows – [here he drew a reflected
> 'S' shape of circles diminishing in size].

Elisabeth Potter was finding it hard to sleep at night after her
brother-in-law had died very suddenly. At the time she was
worried and in bed alone as her husband was abroad:

> I was awake and suddenly aware of a terribly bright
> light – the whole room seemed alight and then I had
> an enormous feeling of peace and [that] everything
> would be alright and [that] I wasn't to worry any
> more. I remember being completely convinced that all
> would be well – I wasn't frightened, just had this
> enormous feeling of relief. Over the years I have tried
> to explain away what happened rationally – stress,
> worry, hallucination, a dream – but I don't think [it
> was any of these].

Reverend Leigh Richardson's encounter came during the long
procedure for training for the Ministry. He had passed the

Diocesan Conference and was in preparation for the three day Provincial Selection Conference. During three months leading up to it he periodically experienced a 'visitation' by something: '... it would come in through the window and hover above my head and then by the window and then disappear. I can only describe it as a fizzy glow!... I knew I wasn't awake when I "saw" this light, but it calmed my fears and helped concentrate my mind.'

However, after the conference the visitations stopped until one night, (as it turned out, it happened to be the night before a letter arrived telling him that he had passed and had been recommended for training) '... it came through the window as usual, but this time there was a finality about it. It seemed to say "My job is done, I have seen you through this testing patch – you no longer need my help" – and it extinguished itself rather than going back through the window. I have never seen it since.'

As Reverend Richardson commented, this experience was subconscious, but it worked in the sense it made him feel 'calmed and confident in what I was doing (giving up teaching to be a priest) – in that it was right and I will always believe that it was my guardian angel helping me through that time, dispelling my fears.'

All in all, experiences that occur during this twilight period, be the recipient wide awake or perhaps without realising it in an altered state of consciousness, are all essentially the same.

UNEXPECTED ENCOUNTERS

'... when I chanced to look upwards. To my amazement, the whole of the upper part of the nave, above the altar, was filled with angels. They were packed up to the top rafters, some superimposed on others, and they had white robes, tinged with gold from the candlelight, and wings outlined in gold.'

M OST ENCOUNTERS WITH angels seem to fit in to one category, be it a vision occurring in the bedroom, a hospital, around death or before, during or after an accident. The following accounts, however, seemed to happen for no reason – they didn't save anyone, give any particular message, help out in any way – they just 'happened', but nonetheless made for powerful and memorable encounters.

Paul Spence writes:

> I was intrigued to read about angelic encounters, of which I have never heard […] before but experienced one when I was about five or six years old.
>
> Of course I did not realise what I was seeing at the time and it looked perfectly natural for the two figures to squeeze through the door with all the other children who were dressed up as fairies and other characters at the school show. They all entered from the corridor at the right and made their entrance on to the stage. Being very young I sat with the others on the floor close up to the stage and could see very clearly when the mother, who was carrying a small baby and dressed in a long white night-dress, went to the back of the stage and sat an a chair facing towards us. The young girl with her, who was dressed the same, knelt at her feet and put her hands together and appeared to pray. She seemed to be about ten or twelve years old. What took my interest was the absence of socks or stockings when she removed her ordinary black shoes and put them neatly to one side. I was captivated by her beautiful white wings, which

Seeing Angels

looked so superior to the cellophane wings of the little
girls dressed as fairies. I could see they were made of
individual white feathers, just like swans' wings, and I
can still marvel at their perfection. I nudged the boy
next to me to look but he didn't seem interested.
Perhaps he couldn't see what I was seeing.

I do not recall seeing any more of them after that. It
must have been years later before I realised what I had
seen and the fact that the figures probably took no part
in the entertainment. I am now just turned seventy and
do not believe in ghosts, spirits, poltergeists or any
other paranormal claptrap.

Lynda Barton was also young when she saw an angel: 'From
1952 to approx. 1965 I lived in a Victorian semi in south-east
London. Whilst playing in the hallway one day, I looked up
the stairs to see a figure clad in white – not ghostly, but with a
calm appearance. I just looked, un-frightened and believed I
had seen an angel and went on with my play.'

Other experiences seem to be even more subtle – such as
the one that Anne Marie Fearon describes. Back in 1979 she
was living in Bristol with her seven-year-old son:

His school was housed in old Pro-Cathedral
buildings... my son and I were standing outside the
school gates. I glanced down the alleyway that ran
along side the school, and before I was conscious of
seeing anything particular I heard myself say 'Good
heavens, there's an angel!' A second later, when my
eyes had focused, I saw a perfectly ordinary human
figure coming towards us up the lane. As he came
nearer I saw a nondescript middle-aged man in a
slightly crumpled grey suit, but as he drew level with

219

us he turned to me and smiled a perfectly angelic
smile, as if he was saying: "Ah, I see you recognised
me! Not everyone does, you know." Then he walked
on.

Not a very dramatic or convincing tale perhaps, but
a striking experience for me since I think I tend to be a
rather controlled and rational person, but the words,
'Good heavens there's an angel' had completely by-
passed my everyday thinking mind. I was not in any
particular stress or danger at the period, and in fact the
whole event seemed rather casual! It didn't seem as if
he was 'sent' to me specially, rather as though he was
on some other errand and I just happened to spot him
passing...

Light

As we have seen previously, some experiences are characterised
by visions of pure light but have been interpreted by the
witnesses as being angelic in nature. Duncan Dale-Emberton's
experience 'happened when I was somewhere between twenty-
six and thirty, and pretty fit despite having undergone massive
chest surgery in 1960 – several months in hospital, during most
of which I was given little chance of survival, and already
classified [as] disabled following Royal Naval service. I have
never told anyone about it, and am doing so now only because
you are involved in theology. I have always been a level-
headed, feet-on-the-ground Christian, brought up on King
James, Cranmer and Hymns A & M, and with a deep, quiet
faith which respects and welcomes other beliefs...'

Early one evening, at a time of year when it was
already dusk, I left the office, in a peaceful little avenue
off a long pedestrian walk, from the other side of

which I was suddenly aware of a light, not tremendously bright but very strong, which seemed to rise above the buildings. The site of the light was also the centre of an enormous power. There were other people around; it was clear that they had noticed nothing of the sort, but I was unable to move until it had 'released' me. I had, and still have, no doubt that it was of a numinous nature, which left me considerably shaken. (As a former boxer and rugby player, I was and am not easily shaken.) I had not been thinking about anything even remotely of the sort before it happened.

The only other thing like it came when I went on holiday to my Dorset home and looked around the family church of the Holy Trinity in Dorchester, which was then Church of England. As I reached the lectern, I was overwhelmingly aware of my father's presence; he had died in 1951, at the age of thirty-six, when I was nine years old, but was certainly there then, all those years later. He had been a lay reader who, when we (the children) were post-first infancy, had let us decide whether we still wanted to attend services. I did.

Alan James Hall wrote how seeing an article relating to this research had interested him 'and jogged my memory – because of something unusual that I saw on New Year's Eve some years ago… in Northumberland.'

To cut a long story short – I was sledging with a friend, Peter Wells, on a hill near where I was living at the time. It was snowing and it was dark – because it was mid-evening. Pete and I had just returned to the top of our 'run' when we saw a very bright golden 'light' appear above a group of mature trees. At first we simply wondered what it was – I assumed that it must have been a helicopter for want of a better explanation. Quickly however, we realised that we couldn't identify it and that we hadn't seen anything like it – also it made no sound. It was about as big as a bus. We weren't scared at all – but I felt 'awed'. The golden light moved at walking pace and the tress behind it indicated that it was only just above their uppermost branches.

Because it was snowing in big flakes, we ran to get closer to it – hoping for a better look at it – this helped up to a point (we got to within eighty yards of it) At this stage it had stopped moving – or it moved very slowly. We could see, even though the falling snow made it difficult, that it was transparent at its 'core', and indistinct shapes could be made out. It also had a tail (like a comet) even though it wasn't moving. I can also remember that the light was steady and not dazzling.

I'm sorry that I can't give you a better description but whatever it was, it was so completely different that I can't think of anything… to compare it with. After a few minutes it moved away so we attempted to follow it on foot by getting onto the road. We saw it lose height for a while – then lost sight of it, even though (because of the hill), we were higher than it.
Well, the 'thing' was so blatantly obvious that we knew other people must have seen it too. So we rushed back to my house fully expecting a 'news flash' on the telly. I thought the world had changed! My wife and Pete's girlfriend already had the television set switched on, and our arrival coincided with the news. The big story was 'lights' seen by the crew and passengers of an airliner… in New Zealand (one of

many 'sightings' as it later turned out). The next day our local paper reported sightings of our light – including policemen who had been eye witnesses. Of course, a UFO was the verdict.

The thing is – I didn't get the impression that it was a machine of some sort – I was convinced that [...] it was a living thing's 'body'. I feel very fortunate to have seen it – whatever it was… also, although I believe that I saw an angel, I am not a religious maniac and I don't think what we saw was remotely interested in us.

Another case of seeing a glowing ball of light occurred to Joan Pritchard when she was working as a teacher in the autumn of 1947. She writes:

I was in lodgings with a friend… during the night when I was in bed, on I think about three or [so] occasions, I saw a glowing ball of light to my left above my head near the ceiling. I sensed that it was something unusual and I remember pulling my head under the clothes and looking again to make sure it was still there. It could not have been a reflection because the window was at the left side of the bed and I was sure that it was something unusual, but I think I felt not afraid but unsure of what to think. As far as I remember I have never seen glowing balls since then…

Carolyn Rogers didn't see balls of light, rather fluttering triangular shapes:

Last October, late on the Saturday night of the half-term week, I went out of my back door, which leads out onto my top terrace patio, to let in my cat, Panda.

To the right of the patio, I experienced a myriad of light movements going up and down in a vertical direction. At first I thought it might be a new kind of laser beaming across from a night-club... so I went inside again. However, before I went upstairs to bed I looked again and then I realised it was not lighting from the club but it must have been a heavenly host of angels. As I looked I felt this incredible sense of awe and excitement, which was a mountain-top experience... Numerically it's difficult to estimate but [there were] certainly in the region of thirty. These fluttering apparitions looked identical, i.e. transparent-white... triangular in shape – there were a pair that were joined in-between by a white shaft of light the width of a broom handle and about the same length. All were exactly the same and they were still there over a period of about thirty minutes, equally placed between each angel, although they were gently moving up and down they were not travelling anywhere, just hovering. I was actually unsure what to do with this experience, what it actually meant – in terms of why to me, and why at that time? I pondered on this for a while... and decided to share my Saturday night experience with my prayer partner, Noreen.

Her grandsons were visiting her at the time and were staying for the half-term holiday break. So we all arranged to go out together for the day... while the children were occupied I tentatively broached the subject of angels and after a hesitant start found myself pouring out the whole experience of last Saturday's sightings! I was utterly amazed to learn that she too had also experienced the same angelic host, though she lives in a different area of the town. It was roughly the same time of evening, 11–12 p.m. Her host was hovering over the Parish Church of St Jude's – the spire which can be seen from her house. Upon reflection we both felt God was trying to say God's glory and favour were over both the church and my hillside home...

Angels at a place of worship

Experiences such as Noreen's came into me in droves, though they tended to occur during services or inside a church. Dena Bryant-Duncan's experience occurred one Christmas:

There was a party of six of us at the service of nine lessons at St Albans Abbey and Cathedral Church in Hertfordshire. It is a very popular service – so much so that they had to issue tickets and even then we had to queue outside for half an hour or so in order to be able to get a seat together. The service is conducted entirely by candlelight, each person having a taper lighted from the main procession in the nave then passed on to a neighbour along the row until the whole congregation, who had been previously seated in the dark, and numbering about two thousand, were now able to see by taper light to sing the carols!

I always enjoy the service; it is one of the highlights of the year. I was, until I moved here five months ago, a regular member of the Abbey Fraternity of Friends, and Flower Guild.

I was following the service, listening to the readings, and singing the carols, when I chanced to look upwards. To my amazement, the whole of the upper part of the nave, above the altar, was filled with angels. They were packed up to the top rafters, some superimposed on others, and they had white robes, tinged with gold from the candlelight, and wings outlined in gold. They were quite still, just listening to the carols and the choir. But also, standing around, some with feet on top of the ancient pews the monks used to sit in, and some high up on window ledges and ancient carvings, were ordinary people, a lot of whom I recognised and realised were 'passed on' – their faces transformed with joy, smiling at us all. I was absolutely overcome. My heart was filled with joy and gladness. It was the best Christmas I have ever had. I told the others in our party and they had seen nothing, but quite believed me.

Monica Devey described seeing two angels together on one occasion and then one of them again at a later date. All of the experiences happened at her old church in Cambridgeshire:

We were having a new church built during the mid-Nineties. The day after the official dedication service, the then Minister... plus others felt there was a lot of oppression in the building, many things were going wrong to stop the completion of the building (it was being done in sections as funding allowed).

It was arranged that a small group of us should go early one Sunday morning to pray in it. Towards the end [...] I saw the two angels behind the communion table. A majestic sight. To describe them, at least eight foot in height, wings outstretched on one, the other folded with the head down. One was the True Angel of Light, the other, The Angel of Righteousness. One would always stay at [the]... church.

Some months later, the following summer during a service one Sunday morning. Being in the music group and seated at one side, ... [the Minister] was talking – his sermon – a glorious day, the sunlight streaming down on him. There appeared the angel, standing behind... [him]

Later, a visitor to our church, on a first visit told [the Minister]... that he too had heard an angel rustling about in the service. [The Minister's wife] was sitting next to me in the music group and knew something had happened, so I told her.

Derek recounted his experience to me over the telephone. His is an ongoing experience that happens whenever he attends Mass. Being an orthodox Catholic, Derek attends church on a very regular basis. At Mass, (during the consecration of the bread especially) he sees 'a whole host of angels hovering above the altar'. Unfortunately Derek finds it hard to talk about this experience, and the fact his story has been ridiculed by the few that he has told it to (including his priest), has unfortunately made his experience one that he would rather not share in full.

Wendy Lawday lived in a small village in Glamorgan during the late Forties to mid-Fifties. She recalls seeing an angel when she was around the age of eight. The village only contains about eight houses, so the church services were sparsely attended, but Wendy would often attend alone if no one else in the family was going...

There was no shop in the village, but one of the villagers – a Mr Durston – used to keep a stock of sweets and ciggies, and occasionally my father would send me to his house for supplies. Dusk was falling as I set off on this particular evening, and as I passed the little church, I noticed a faint flickering light showing through the arched window facing the lane. At first I assumed it was the old lady who used to take care of the church – Mrs. Mathews – but then I saw, silhouetted against the lighted window, what looked to me like an angel with long wings, just as you see in the paintings. The wings moved slightly, and I was absolutely convinced there was an angel inside the church. There seemed to be a glow around the figure, slightly brighter than the rest of the light showing. The background light had a similar effect to an oil or gas lamp – shadowy and flickering, but not bright like electricity.

I ran quickly to Mr Durston's house and said 'there's an angel in the church'. He smiled and said it must be Mrs Mathews, but I dragged him outside to look. When we got to the church – only a few yards from his house – it was in darkness, and there was no sign of Mrs Mathews there – in fact, she was in her house (next door to his) and had not been in the church at the time.

I have never forgotten this experience, but I am afraid I rarely go to church these days. I certainly wish I still had that sweet innocence and faith, because whether the sighting was real or imaginary (and I am sure it was real), looking back on it I realise I was very, very lucky to have witnessed such a thing.

I am afraid the adults chuckled indulgently, but even now when I visit the village I still feel a tingle in the spine when I look at that window.

RESULTS

SO WE HAVE discussed the various accounts and seen a range of different situations and settings in which people have reported encounters with angels; but what are the basic findings from this research? Many questions are raised when talking about and looking at angel visions and experiences. Are all recipients religious? If not, did they gain faith from their encounter? What seems to be the common age for experiences to happen and are they more frequent with women than men? Do different people's experiences have things in common – did all occur when the recipient was in danger, or after they had asked for guidance or did they happen in specific places (such as the bedroom)? What do the angels look like and, following E.B. Tylor's argument in his book Primitive Culture[1], does this tie in with peoples' preconceptions and the media images. Does the image of the angel tie in with what the recipients' culture has constructed for them? Are they culturally determined? How many people actually believe in angels and think that they have an effect on our lives? And why do some people have angelic experiences while others do not? People have written to me describing an angelic intervention that prevented them experiencing a horrific accident, but countless unfortunates die in tragic circumstances every day. Some questions cannot be answered; the ones that can follow.

How the results were affected

As in any census or survey, it is important to bear in mind that these results, although they give us some grasp on a very nebulous area, are not written in stone; nor are they necessarily absolute for the entire UK population. They are taken from 350 self-selecting individuals who chose to respond to my

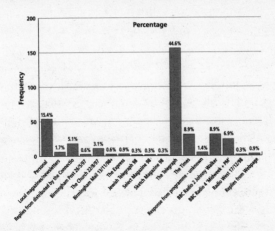

plea. Even so, the similarities between many of them were incredible.

So, from the various articles placed and radio programmes that included a contact address to write to me, who replied to what? And from scanning these results, is it possible to roughly gauge the social status of respondents? Most of the articles were written by the broadsheets which, of course, has a knock-on effect to my data. Therefore, it's important to bear in mind that we are not looking at a complete cross-section of British society. For example, more people read *The Telegraph* than would listen to Radio WM. It is also worth bearing in mind that I never appealed for cases in any of the tabloids such as *The Sun* – where I would imagine the responses would have differed considerably.

Another thing to remember is that from the outset of this research I wore the weighty tag of academia around my neck. Apart from the initial 'Have you seen an angel?' adverts, all other articles mentioned the research was connected to the University of Birmingham. I think if I had have done this research for personal use, or indeed for the sole purpose of writing this book,

I would be working with a different set of data. The university added validity and credence to my work – the broadsheets became interested and published interviews and accounts of it; other papers and magazines did the same. I have been and am invited onto various radio programmes and talk shows to discuss the work. I certainly do not believe things would have taken off so much had I have done this out of personal interest. Moreover, the fact a redbrick university was allowing such research, let alone funding it, instilled more interest.

On the other hand, the university tag could well have hampered respondents. Academia is a world from which some people perhaps feel too removed, and therefore avoid. To some, the stigma is still rife so far as to believe that academics set out to disprove all hypotheses and theories, whilst others simply do not understand exactly what a 'PhD' or a 'thesis' is, let alone what it entails. I corresponded on three different occasions with one gentleman with whom before he divulged his experience. Fortunately, for me it was worth it, but from his point of view he wanted to know my credentials, genuineness and for what exactly I would be using his account. I imagine some people may have assumed my sole purpose was to explain away their experience. This never was, (nor is) on my agenda. I am not a psychiatrist, psychologist nor am I interested in the philosophy of such accounts.

Some questions we can mull over for eternity: are there angels? Do they really exist? I don't know. I am interested in people today – the here and now – some of whom believe they have seen an angel, or in some way, that an angelic figure has touched their life. Do any of these accounts have common factors? Are they all religious? Are they elderly? Whereabout in the UK did respondents live? Were there certain locations, or certain mind-sets, in which an experience tended to occur? These were the key areas of my interest – whether angels exist or not is irrelevant; the belief in them and the sociological impact as a result of them, however, is not.

Where the respondents live

Just as who replied to what article has a bearing on the data, where they live can also give us an impression of who is reporting such experiences and where. At first look at this, a horrific front-page headline appears in my mind: 'North-South Divide hits again – Southerners more likely to have Angel Experiences' – with people making pilgrimages to the south-east to go and angel watch. (As silly as it sounds, it happened with U.F.O. sightings and alien abductions.) This is most definitely not the case here – please bear in mind the denser population in the south-east and the places articles were taken from! Moreover, the media in which this study was advertised in are individually more prevalent in certain areas, which again affects the data.

After flicking through various divisional maps of the British Isles I opted to use the Central Statistical Office's Regional Profiles[2] as, unlike the various counties, these divisions are stable ones and also consist of less division which make analysis and cross-referencing easier.

For the purpose of this work then, Great Britain is divided into eleven categories as follows:

1. SCOTLAND – Highland, Grampian, Tayside, Central, Fife, Lothian, Strathclyde, Borders and Dumfries and Galloway.
2. THE NORTH – Northumberland, Cumbria, Durham, Tyne and Wear and Cleveland
3. THE NORTH-WEST – Lancashire, Merseyside, Greater Manchester and Cheshire.
4. YORKSHIRE AND HUMBERSIDE – North Yorkshire, West Yorkshire, South Yorkshire and Humberside.

5 WALES – Clwyd, Gwynedd, Powys, Dyfed, West Glamorgan, Mid Glamorgan, South Glamorgan and Gwent.
6 IRELAND
7 WEST MIDLANDS – Staffordshire, Shropshire, West Midlands, Hereford and Worcestershire and Warwickshire.
8 EAST MIDLANDS – Derbyshire, Nottinghamshire, Lincolnshire, Leicestershire, Northamptonshire.
9 EAST ANGLIA – Norfolk, Cambridgeshire, Suffolk.
10 THE SOUTH-WEST – Gloucestershire, Avon, Wiltshire, Somerset, Dorset, Devon and Cornwall.
11 THE SOUTH-EAST – Oxfordshire, Bedfordshire, Bucks, Herts, Essex, Berkshire, Greater London, Kent, Surrey, Hampshire, West Sussex, East Sussex, Isle of Wight.

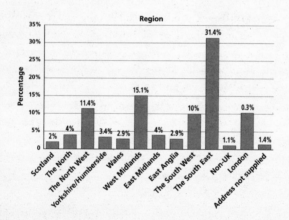

'I have not spoken about this for over forty years now...'

To many, religious experience remains immensely personal. This is apparent in the fact that, in some cases, I have been privileged enough to be one of the few people with whom the respondents have shared their angelic experience:

at the time [after the experience] I was too shocked to
share the experience with even my family, and ever
since have only told it to a few

the experience I relate is a one-off thing for me, and is
something I only ever shared with my husband. This
is because it is very personal and special, not because I
doubt its authenticity

I have told very few people of this experience as it's so
very precious to me, but wanted you to maybe include
it in your research

To a modicum of recipients, I am apparently the first person to
have been told of their otherworldly encounter – a reason for
this may be because of a fear of being disbelieved or even
ridiculed. Some described that hearing about this research was
a relief to them, as it meant that they were not alone in seeing
or experiencing what they had.

This was unfortunately the case for one Catholic gentleman
with whom I shared a telephone conversation. He discussed
multiple experiences of seeing angels hovering above the altar
whilst at Mass. He subsequently informed me that he regrets
mentioning it, however, as he has was instantly labelled a
'loony' by the rest of the congregation and even by the priest,
thus making it an experience he rather wished he had not
shared. Fortunately, this was the only negative account I have
been told – though it is understandable that sightings can, by
some, be taken the wrong way.

Negative angel experiences
I have received few unpleasant, or 'negative', angelic
experiences; in fact, the number you could count on one hand.

We have all heard about fallen angels and bad angels. This could well be an area of research in its own right, probably equally as large as productive angelic experiences. However, I have not really had to deal with any such data. Perhaps this is tied in with the problem we have with language: if someone sees a positive, calming presence it is attributed to an angel; if that presence were in any way evil or eerie would it necessarily have angelic connotations? I think not – would one not call a figure encountered in such a context a devil or a ghost? This begs the question: is there such a thing as a negative angel experience? An experience that leaves the recipient wishing they had never had it? Left them fearful and afraid? As yet, the evidence does not appear to suggest so.

Age at time of experience

Of all the categories, this is one of the most surprising. In it there is a proportion within each age bracket created – interestingly the majority being in the 31–50 band. Arguments for this though must be born in mind – looking back to the

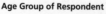

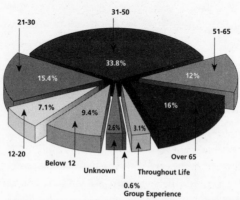

Age Group of Respondent

31-50 33.8%
21-30 15.4%
51-65 12%
16%
7.1%
9.4%
2.6%
3.1%
12-20
Below 12
Unknown
Throughout Life
Over 65
0.6%
Group Experience

reply codes, many responded to an article in *The Telegraph*, a paper with a readership that is perhaps weighty with this generation. The same goes for the radio programmes and shows that were responded to.

Faith

Under this heading I have provided a breakdown of the respondents' faith – although the vast majority are Christian, we need to put in proportion the fact that many of the respondents wrote after seeing articles and adverts in the religious press, which took interest in this work. Also, when seeing the headline, people with an interest in angels are more likely to read the words below it than someone with no interest.

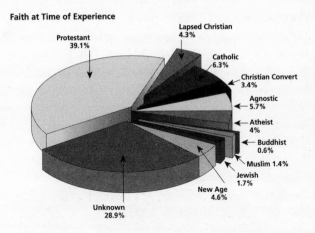

Faith at Time of Experience

- Protestant 39.1%
- Lapsed Christian 4.3%
- Catholic 6.3%
- Christian Convert 3.4%
- Agnostic 5.7%
- Atheist 4%
- Buddhist 0.6%
- Muslim 1.4%
- Jewish 1.7%
- New Age 4.6%
- Unknown 28.9%

It is apparent that people from all cultures, backgrounds and faiths relate fundamentally the same types of experience. As I write, nothing concrete has been written cross culturally. Perhaps there is a reason for this? Maybe there is in fact nothing to actually report? Today there are myriad religions sharing similar philosophies yet participating in dissimilar rituals and beliefs. Angels are, in a way, an umbrella over them all – they are an entity shared across all the mainstream religions, including Christianity, Judaism, Islam and Zoroastrianism. Indeed, Bodhisattvas fulfil the same role in Buddhism, as avatars do in Hinduism. It is also apparent from this work that agnostics and atheists have the same kinds of experiences as believers in orthodox religions.

The angelic role is most fully elaborated in religions based on revelation, such as Zoroastrianism, Judaism, Christianity, and Islam. All of these religions are monotheistic (worship only one god) and emphasise the distance between man and God, therefore having the greatest need for intermediaries to span the gap. Conversely, in polytheistic religions (those in which more than one god is worshipped) the gap between humankind and their deities is far less pronounced and angelic functions are often performed by one of the gods in a human form (i.e. their role is less pronounced). So, spiritual beings akin to angels do exist within both monotheistic and polytheistic faiths; they almost unilaterally exist to facilitate a rapport between the worshipper and the worshipped. An example is the Chinese shen who are benevolent spirits, often interpreted as the ghosts of ancestors who, through appropriate rituals, can be appropriated into the service of the living. In Shinto, the kami are the spirits of deities, ancestors, and even a number of natural objects, whose favour and help are won by reverence and pious obedience. Japanese Buddhists consider the kami to be manifestations of the gods, or bodhisattvas.

Type of angel seen across the different faiths

It is interesting to note that the traditional-style angel is the vision most regularly reported, across the faiths, and also fascinating to see that none of the four Muslims who wrote to me saw this type of angel. Instead they saw an angel in human form and smelt a scent, while two heard an audible voice.

Fig.7	Statistics of Angel Form – Based on Simplified Replies								
Faith at Experience	Traditional Style	Human Form	Scent	Light	Audible Noise	Physical Sensation	Internal Sensation	Other attributes	Total
Christian Convert	4			5	2	1			12
Agnostic	7	6	2		1	1	1	2	20
Atheist	4	1	1	3	1	1		2	13
Buddhist	1					1			2
Muslim		2	1		2				5
Jewish	2				1	1		2	6
New Age	9		1	1	2	1	1	1	16
Protestant	37	29	8	17	7	18	8	13	137
Lapsed Christian	10		3	1				1	15
Catholic	7	5	2	2	1	3		2	22
Unknown	28	16	16	14		6	7	14	102
Total	109	59	34	44	17	33	17	37	350

However, such small figures do not, of course, provide us with a complete overview of the representation of angels for the worshippers of Islam. Far from it.

I would have loved to have spent more time researching angelic experiences within each separate differing faith community. Perhaps these could be topics for someone else in the future. There is much more work on this area still to be undertaken.

Where the experience happened

The questions thrown up by these results are vast. As discussed in chapter ten, the most common place for an experience appears to be in the bedroom, a location natually sympathetic to notions of altered states of consciousness and, of course, vivid dreams.

Other sites in which an angelic encounter occurred include a hospital, at home around the house, outside, during or after an accident, in a place of worship (a church, synagogue, temple and so forth), in another building or on transport (such as in a car, on a train or plane).

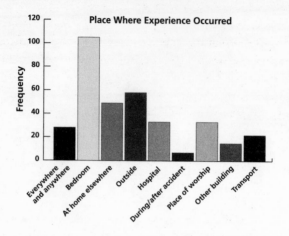

Type of angel seen by men and women

It is interesting to break the statistics up and look more closely at what men and women saw. Bearing in mind, statistically there were just over 100% more women in the numbers, one should roughly double the appearances seen by men to get a better picture. Even so, in ratio more women reported seeing an angel in traditional form, and more men saw the angel in human form. The reports of scent, light and audible noises are about even between the sexes, as is a physical and internal sensation, though more men attributed 'other attributes' (such

Statistics of Angel Form x Sex of Respondent			
	Female	Male	Total
Traditional Style Angel	87	22	109
Human Form	36	23	59
Scent	25	9	34
Light	28	16	44
Audible Noise	12	5	17
Physical Sensation	22	11	33
Internal Sensation	12	5	17
Other Attributes	21	16	37
Total	243 = 69%	107 = 31%	350

as seeing a ghostly apparition or feeling an evil presence) as being angelic in nature.

The place where the experience occurred is pretty similar between the sexes (again, double the figure in the male column to get a rough estimate of what it would be had the respondents been divided equally between male and female). The figures are roughly equal and what we would expect. The only one that stands out is experiences at the time of an accident or just afterwards – this type of experience is more common in men.

The after-effect of the experience

As can be seen throughout all the differing experiences recounted, there are common factors between the different individual experiences. However, the impact of the experience on the recipient's life also has common factors. Others in this field have also noted, as this study has shown, 'All describe a

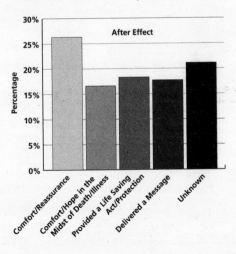

The After Effect of the Experience

Experience provided general comfort/reassurance	26%
Experience occurred around death/terminal illness providing hope	17%
Experience occurred as a life-saving act/prevention from accident	18%
Experience delivered a message	18%
No particular after-effect felt	21%

wonderful elation, peace and lightness of spirit that a brush of an angel's wing leaves lingering in the air. A feeling of illuminating inner-change is the true hallmark of an encounter with an angel. You can never again view the world in the same way'.[3]

The after-effect of such visions surrounding death and dying

I feel this is worth a separate mention, as this category incorporates (in some cases) the receiving of a message and visions around a death – thus combining many experiences together. According to the data received for death experiences, the after-effect of all the encounters has been comfort, reassurance, and hope – not just to the person who had the experience initially, but to other family members, and friends who have been told about it. Some visions involved being asked to give a message from a loved one to somebody else; alternatively, the message may have been intended for them, perhaps as a warning or prediction. The most frequent messages from deceased loved ones, expressed verbally or non-verbally, tended to all be along the lines of: 'I'm OK... Don't worry about me. Don't grieve for me... Please let me go... I'm happy... I'm watching over you.' In such cases, the roles of guardian angel, spirit guide and ghost become merged, a definite shift in terminology and meaning that is happening today.

One much-debated question at this time is whether spiritual

visions can help in resolving grief or preventing pathological grief. Leading authorities in near-death studies, such as Maggie Callahan and Elizabeth Kubler Ross, have presented anecdotes or stories documenting that spiritual visions heal grief. Reading accounts from chapter nine, 'Angels of Death', that certainly appears to be the case with angel visions and experiences. As some respondents described being utterly obliterated by the grief, they still find and are able to achieve spiritual growth from ADCs and after seeing that they were not alone on their journey to the next plane. It seems such visions certainly have their place along the healing path.

As Melvin Morse[4] has found, mainstream medical science has not even begun to try to understand if spiritual visions can help those who are struggling to come to terms with the death of someone they love. Virtually every recent mainstream social science, nursing or medical text on grieving stoutly ignores even the existence of spiritual visions in the context of death and dying. Therese Rando's excellent text, *The Parental Loss of a Child*, for example, only briefly mentions that many parents have vivid hallucinations after the death of a child, of that child. Why is this? Will things slowly start to change?

Each and every experience that has been reported to me has some sort of effect and seems to be interpreted by the witness dependent on their individual needs. Experiences seem to have a corrective effect on the witness's life: for example, if the person was severely ill, the angelic presence either assisted their recovery in a physical way, or enabled them to accept their condition, or alleviated their suffering completely (as well as the suffering of their next of kin) in a spiritual way. If the person was afraid, then comfort was offered; if the person was in a life-threatening situation, the angelic intervention frequently saved their life.

Not all experiences were necessarily dramatic as might have

perhaps been originally envisaged when contemplating angelic experiences. Some were perhaps so subtle that the majority of people would tend to overlook them, but those who attributed them to being brought about by an angel seem to have gained much more out of the experience that others who may have been more dismissive of it.

TENTATIVE
CONCLUSIONS

SEEING, HEARING AND being touched by an angel (metaphorically or literally) tends to happen to people on a personal basis. Simply because one has not had personal experience of such a phenomenon does not mean it does not exist. One cannot literally see the wind, though its effects can be observed and measured and its outcome felt. That is precisely how I see the angel phenomenon and my place studying it. I am merely observing and writing about this present-day social phenomenon. I certainly have never been out to promote the veracity of the heavenly kingdom nor try and 'sell' the notion of angels to people.

Scepticism: truth versus reality – angels and science

While participating in the BBC Everyman documentary about this study, I recall Norman Hull, the programme's director stating that he 'makes films about the *truth*, not about *reality*'. Indeed, when people hear about this research, they are quick to ask 'Do you think angels are real, then?' The purpose has never been to try and prove or disprove angelic existence – such a task is neither possible nor of any interest to me. I am solely concerned with the social aspect – the surge of interest, the people who report having had such experiences, the way they describe and talk about them and the effect it has upon their lives. So, to coin a phrase, my work and this book is not about 'reality' – it is about is the 'truth' of what is going on and possible explanations as to why – why angels, why now? And people wrote to me in their hundreds, providing testimonies outlining their unique experience, their faith system and the after-effect it's had on their lives.

Countless times I have been told by sceptics that the concept of angels is not scientifically credible. However, we must take into account that although we have had a few hundred years' of science, science far from explains logical answers to everything. Dr Fraser Watts of the University of Cambridge explained to me that we are still in the foothills of science – still learning each day. Even now we have no idea how relativity theory and quantum physics can be connected, which in turn may well give credence to the possibility of angelic beings.

The arguments regarding modernity drive me mad too – this blinkered approach states that humans are understanding the 'truth' more and more as they years go by. Such a linear approach insists that human intelligence is increasing – which is true, and not true at the same time. Indeed, knowledge is increasing, but we are also losing contact with intuitive ways of knowing things – as fast as we are learning new things, we are losing grasp of others.

In the book *Physics of Angels*, Matthew Fox (a radical theologian) and Rupert Sheldrake (a radical biologist) put forward a chapter on Thomas Aquinas. Although I don't want to delve too deep into this subject here, there are a few aspects of their study I would like to share. Aquinas was an astonishing thinker and the quality of his intellect is remarkable; indeed many of his ideas seem to be anticipating early physics. Fox discusses the probability and complexity of angelic entities and Aquinas states their 'movement place to place is a succession of power contacts – an angel is not in any place at any one time'[1] – in essence there is no time interval.

So lets take it then that angels are a *possibility*. Who am I after all to assert that such experiences are all in the mind? As previously mentioned, evidence is not conclusive either way and I simply don't believe that the all those people who have written to me outlining their experiences have neurological, mental illnesses or undiagnosed temporal lobe epilepsy!

Are people's preconceptions of angels reflected in their experience?

Following E.B. Tylor's argument in his book *Primitive Culture*[2] that people see what they expect to see, does an angel's appearance tie in with the general preconceptions and media images of these extraordinary otherworldly figures? In response to replies contained within the survey it seems that this is indeed true.

A small survey I carried out a few years back at the University of Birmingham[3] went out randomly to two parishes (one Anglican, one Catholic) and three workplaces; the balance of male to female and their age brackets were almost balanced, obtaining a wide scope of different beliefs and attitudes.

Results from this survey revealed that the majority of people perceived angels as being the Victorian image of a 'traditional-style' angel, 'very serene and gentle' with 'a bright radiant face' and 'huge wings clasped behind her back'. The next most popular image was that of an angel in human form 'like you and me', 'people who go about doing good things and putting the world to right but making no fuss about doing so'. A few wrote that they imagine angels to be a 'spiritual presence' or 'the spirit of a deceased relative' with one person claiming that he believes angels have 'no one identity, they take on which ever appearance is appropriate at the time'. Others, however, left my question about the angel's appearance blank, stating that they were not able to visualise such a creature, using explanations such as 'humans can not comprehend their awe and power' or 'can not attempt to imagine'.

Therefore, it seems that the results from this question in my survey reinforce the percentage of people who saw different images of angels in their experiences, with the majority seeing a traditional-style angel with wings (31%), a human form that disappeared (17%), a light (13%), a scent (10%) or an internal/external feeling (9% for each).

British attitudes towards angels

Perhaps the angel craze should not come as such a great surprise. I often refer to the analogy of the spiritual shopper – consumers walking the isles of the 'Spiritual Supermarket' plucking whichever religions they choose off the shelf – a taste of yoga, some Jewish mysticism, a read of the Kabalah, New Testament or Koran, a touch of Buddhism, a flavour of angels and so forth.

The decline in mainstream faiths and the appeal of picking one's own eclectic religion has a certain appeal to contemporary society, a trend that echoes George Ritzer's theory of the McDonaldisation of society.[4] Ritzer argues that society is fast taking on the values of the McDonald's food chain. He outlines the four main features of both as being efficiency (such as the production line, organisation and an increase of efficiency), quantity (number of people through the door, quantity of product sold with quantity becoming the second-biggest priority) predictability (customers know the layout, the menu – they know what to expect) and non-human contact (voice machine at the Drive Thru, automated tills, computers and other modern technology). It is relatively easy to expand this argument to include religion. I wrote a paper in my undergraduate days suggesting that the contemporary Church was perhaps subconsciously following such a model. This is particularly true in the case of the fast-growing fundamentalist evangelical wing of the church in America, which has essentially taken on exactly such a model: one preacher can stand in a TV studio and reach out to every state. In terms of capital, it's efficient, the sheer quantity of followers is vast and there is a certain sense of predictability in that you can almost guarantee the same clichés, miracles, stories and format of service. The non-human element is there too, in that followers are dealing with the internet or a TV screen not actually being face to face with a preacher. I think we could (albeit loosely) do the same with religion today. People want something – spirituality, relaxation, a purpose in life, but they do not want the aggravation of having to read up on it, learn about it, talk about it – they want the end result and they want it now. One only needs to type 'angel' on an internet search engine to almost instantly have everything angel-related at our fingertips, from chat rooms to esoteric information; we need only pick up the telephone and we can have a prediction from the angel cards.

Although as yet there are no official statistics for the UK, we know that more than three-quarters of Americans believe that angels exist and have an effect on people's lives. But what about other spiritual entities, such as Satan and the Holy Spirit? According to a new nation-wide survey of American adults[5], a large majority of adults do not believe that either the Devil or the Holy Spirit exist.

Nearly two out of three adults – 62% agreed – that Satan 'is not a living being but is a symbol of evil.' This response remained relatively consistent throughout the Nineties. Among the more surprising findings, however, are that a majority of born-again Christians deny Satan's existence (52%); nearly three-quarters of Catholics say the Devil is non-existent (72%); and women are more likely than men to reject Satan's existence (64% of women versus 59% of men).

Perhaps the most stunning result of the survey, though, is the nation's conclusion that there is no such thing as the Holy Spirit. Six out of ten Americans (61%) agreed that 'the Holy Spirit is a symbol of God's presence or power, but is not a living entity.' In the Christian faith, which 84% of all adults claim to embrace, the Holy Spirit is part of the Trinity, which is the expression of God in three persons. Among the segments of the population most likely to deny the existence of the Holy Spirit were Baby Busters (i.e. adults 18 to 31 years old, of whom 66% rejected the Spirit) and non-whites (66%). Amazingly, a majority of all born-again

Christians also reject the existence of the Holy Spirit (55%).[6]

I would query how this question was phrased, given the data – it seems somewhat improbable. However, the results do display a clear example of how people are picking and choosing their beliefs. Alone, the fact that individuals might choose to leave out the Holy Spirit and Satan but to include angels and call themselves, be it nominally or not, Christians astounds me. Others take it further and call themselves 'New Age' or 'agnostic/atheist' and simply ascribe to a belief in angels.

Responses from the quantitative survey I collated showed that 70% of people believe that angels do exist, which complements the survey carried out by *Time Magazine* (referred to in the introduction), which found that 69% of American people believed in angels.

The percentages were above average for all the questions on the survey – 70% believing angels exist, 62% believing they influence people's lives and 64% believing that some people can talk and see angels.

However, it is a known fact that women are more likely to put pen to paper than men. The BBC, for example, receives a higher percentage of correspondence from women than men – be it critical or complimentary in nature. This was exemplified by the letters that I received outlining individual angelic experiences – only one in three accounts was from a man (33% men to 67% women). However, the results from the qualitative survey were surprising in that a high percentage of men attested to a belief in angels (38% compared with just 32% women), although they were more sceptical when it came to belief in angels influencing people's lives (24%) and believing that some people can see and communicate with angels (22%).

Why the sudden surge of interest?

If angelic experiences are on the increase what implication does this have for our society? What is the root of the sudden interest in angels at the present? Some would argue that the approach of the millennium accounted for a large part of the spiritual boom. As Glennyce Eckersly points out:

> An entire generation of people has been brought up without any kind of religion and angels could be the manifestation of our need for spiritual fulfilment. Lots of people talk about having lucky escapes and now some of those people may attribute it to having a guardian angel. Others may be using their intuition about something and putting it down to a guardian angel talking to them.[7]

There are numerous websites[8] currently in operation that are based on the subject of angels and the circulation of various angelic encounters, stories and literature is accessible to people all around the globe. What was once more or less a taboo area, or at least not something associated with 'normal' people, is becoming more and more widely known. In doing so, a more accepting atmosphere is created that others may enter into and share their experiences.

In *The Golden Bough*, Frazer put forward the theory that we have passed through three eras: those of magic, religion and science. With the move between each one there was a certain amount of overlap – this idea would suggest that we are currently between the religion and science era, ebbing more towards science. I would expand on and create another model based on this concept of eras to suggest there has been a cycle of phases. Paranormal phenomena seem to become more or less fashionable in cycles – we had the bad or frightening ghosts of the pre-Victorian era; the late 19th century saw a preoccupation with the subject of fairies. Although belief in poltergeists was still apparent in the 20th century, other forms of spirits were viewed as less threatening and harmless. During the late 20th century there emerged a fixation with aliens, alien abductions and UFOs. As platform shoes or bootleg trousers keep coming back, so do other trends – perhaps it is simply that now, once again, the angel wave has arisen. Going back to Frazer's model, it could be argued that we are presently in the 'good ghost'/ 'angel' phase, and it is this overlap that is creating a merging of angels and ghosts in people's minds. It certainly appears that many people who are having angel experiences see deceased relatives and I find it fascinating to see the shift in language that runs GHOST – SPIRIT – ENERGY – ANGEL.

Can all experiences be legitimately explained away?

Delving into the way of thinking in psychiatric phenomenology it would stand to reason that that some of the experiences people recall may not be based in reality. As discussed in the introduction, there is more than one explanation for an angelic experience. In *Cosmopolitan*, Dr Susan Blackmore argues that 'when the body is in pain or shock, your inhibitory cells stop working and your body releases endorphins, which bring on hallucinations and feelings of blissfulness. Then a person's visual cortex is affected and cells start firing off all over the place which could explain... bright lights. One thing scientists know for sure is we all have a temporal lobe which, when stimulated, gives a tingling sensation or the appearance of a bright light – how people choose to interpret it comes and goes. Angels are the trend at the moment.'[9]

This type of explanation may be valid for experiences that were induced from a life-threatening scenario (such as being trapped on cliffs, being run over by a lorry, nearly drowning in the sea or the prospect of being in a head-on collision), but what if the experience was in response to a prayer asking for protection, or those experiences that helped people suffering with severe illness? What about experiences that seemingly predicted and foretold events, such as births or deaths? What psychological explanation can be given for experiences that seemingly happen without reason? And how can experiences that occurred as a 'helping hand' be explained according to this theory? Could such cases suggest that there is a spiritual world beyond our own earthly existence?

A sceptic may argue that reports of angels taking part in dramatic rescues or chaotic, emotional experiences, were recorded by individuals with a fertile mind who may have seized upon such a suppressed image in a bid to reduce their panic. But when disaster happens suddenly, in many cases before the person actually realised the danger they were in, does this theory really hold tight?

There are so many theories that can be used to counter an individual's assertion that he or she has seen an angel. Take those experiences that were reported to have occurred in the bedroom, for instance. The twilight state is the first obvious theory to discount the experience. The experience occurred – no one is disputing that – the dispute is what it was caused by, a physical angelic entity or something within us. The twilight state is a level of consciousness that can be attained by various relaxation techniques, including meditation exercises, hypnosis, and deep prayer. Such angelic experience that happen either on waking or going to sleep – referred to by psychopathologists as the hypnopompic and hypnogogic stages respectively – are the times when people are most likely to experience hallucinations, generally auditory in nature. About 60% of the population have had this kind of experience, so it is not uncommon. Some attribute it to being their guardian angel, others to the presence of a deceased relative, others to both and some simply dismiss it, believing it to be their minds working overtime!

How, though, do we explain experiences that seemingly happened spontaneously – without thought or action? Did all of these people suddenly awake in such a state receptive to visions? As it happens, much of my data is of this nature – experiences happening, for want of a better phrase, out of the blue. As explained in the introduction – the sceptics would try to explain away the experiences as hallucination, daydream, hysteria or mind projection. Medical explanations might include undiagnosed schizophrenia, especially in the case of hearing voices; but we must remember that these are not repeated voices that circle round in people's heads – they are usually one-off messages or warnings.

One valid theory I do take seriously, however, is the idea of altered states of consciousness. In *The Complete Book of Aliens and Abduction*[10], Jenny Randles proposes a state of consciousness that is the converse of lucid dreaming – for example, that instead of knowing you're asleep and being able to control your dreaming, you are awake but open to uncontrolled dream-like experiences – whether they be of an alien abduction or an angelic vision or encounter. Because you know you're awake, and because the experience is so vivid, the recipient would swear blind that it was real, even if it opens them up to ridicule.

Randles also refers[11] to much academic work that has been carried out by Barber & Wilson (1983), Myers & Austrin (1985), Lynn & Rhue (1987) and others on 'fantasy prone personalities' – people with strongly visual memories who are apparently more likely to be abducted, have visions, near-death experiences and the like, and are unusually good hypnotic regression subjects (with all that that implies for supposed abductions, past lives and Satanic ritual –or any other – abuse).

On the other side of the coin, theoretical physics and recent advances in mathematics suggest at least two other realities, in theory. Mathematician Michio Kaku, in his book *Hyperspace*[12], states that it is not hard to scientifically describe other realities. He feels the problem is in understanding how we access or communicate with them.

Recent medical research indicates that we are all born with a sixth sense, located in our right temporal lobe, which allows us to perceive spiritual realities. Furthermore, electromagnetic sensing devices of unknown use have also been discovered in our brains. I am not suggesting that mainstream medicine currently accepts all of this. But our current medical and scientific world model is rapidly changing. Our ability to understand and study spiritual visions has rapidly progressed from pseudoscience to science in the past ten years. Studies from such seemingly unrelated areas as the National Warfare Institute, and the Brain Surgery Research Group at the University of California in San Diego have all contributed pieces of Melvin Morse's theory that humans beings are genetically programmed to see and interact with other realities using their right temporal lobe.[13]

The future for angels

And so the book comes full circle. The wave of interest in angels has still not crashed. Will angels simply be a fad – albeit a longer-lasting one than NDEs, aliens and UFOs? Will they lose their appeal and be taken over by something else equally as quirky? Whether the interest wanes or increases, these experiences are real to the people who have them and leave a great and lasting impression on their lives. Sadly, although many taboos have been and are being broken down, the whole area of religious experience is still a grey area and remains something that many find hard to openly discuss.

Things are changing – slowly. Firstly, it is apparent that elements from New Age beliefs (such as spirit guides, relatives becoming angels) are being interwoven with the mainstream faiths. I return to the analogy mentioned earlier of the 'spiritual shopping basket'. This basket is enabling more and more people to pick and mix and therefore choose their own eclectic 'religious' (for want of a better word) philosophies and ideas.

I think the belief surrounding angels today held by a surprisingly high number of people can be summed up in the well-known words of Robbie Williams's hit single 'Angels'. Just like popping an aspirin, this idea is worryingly starting to stick. Whether because of global McDonaldization or for myriad other reasons, people are simply 'loving angels instead' – for how much longer though, only time will tell.

Angels are perceived harmless. To believe in angels and follow them you need not follow any commandments – you can pick them up and leave them alone at will. Angels are seen as forces of good, as comforting. In life-threatening situations, they are seen as calming and providers of hope and reassurance. To associate one's deceased grandmother with being a lifelong guardian is not a radically new idea, but different philosophies, faiths and ideas are being merged all the time...

Make of these findings what you will. As any theologian (or scientist, for that matter) would declare, one does not prove the existence of anything by simply giving it a name or indeed writing a book on it. All I have done here is relay my findings and record the encounters people have passed onto me. With this in mind, I feel it best to leave you with a dictum laid down by the medieval philosopher William of Ockham – that in giving explanations, one should make the fewest assumptions.

I really don't believe the world is purely physical – there is much we still do not know nor understand. In the words of Hamlet:

There are more things in heaven and earth, Horatio,
Than are dreamt of in your philosophy... [14]

APPENDIX (i)

Angels on screen

Always (1989), Richard Dreyfuss, John Goodman, Audrey Hepburn, and Holly Hunter.

Angels in the Outfield (1951), Paul Douglas, Janet Leigh.

The Angel Levine (1970), Zero Mostel and Harry Belafonte.

The Angel Who Pawned Her Harp (1954), Diane Cilento, Felix Aylmer.

The Bishop's Wife (1947), Cary Grant, Loretta Young, David Niven.

Cabin in the Sky (1943), Eddie Anderson, Ethel Waters.

Charley and the Angel (1973), Fred MacMurray, Cloris Leachman, Harry Morgan, KurtRussell.

City of Angels (1998), Nicolas Cage, Meg Ryan.

Clarence (1991), Robert Carradine, Kate Trotter.

Date with an Angel (1987), Emmanuelle Béart, Michael E. Knight.

Faraway, So Close! (1993), Otto Sander, Peter Falk.

For Heaven's Sake (1950), Clifton Webb, Joan Bennett.

Forever Darling (1956), Lucille Ball, Desi Arnaz, James Mason.

Green Pastures (1936), Rex Ingram, Eddie Anderson.

A Guy Named Joe (1943), Spencer Tracy, Irene Dunne.

Heaven Can Wait (1978), Warren Beatty, Jack Warden, Dyan Cannon.

Heaven Only Knows (1947), Robert Cummings, Brian Donlevy.

The Heavenly Kid (1985), Lewis Smith, Jason Gedrick.

Here Comes Mr. Jordan (1941), Robert Montgomery, Claude Rains, Evelyn Keyes.

The Horn Blows at Midnight (1945), Jack Benny, Alexis Smith.

Human Feelings (1978), Billy Crystal, Nancy Walker.

I Married an Angel (1942), Jeanette MacDonald, Nelson Eddy.

It's a Wonderful Life (1946), Jimmy Stewart, Donna Reed.

The Kid with the Broken Halo (1982), Gary Coleman, Robert Guillaume.

Michael (1996), John Travolta, William Hurt.

Mr. Destiny (1990), James Belushi, Linda Hamilton.

The Prophecy (1995), Christopher Walken.

The Seventh Sign (1988), Demi Moore, Michael Biehn, JŸrgen Prochnow.

Two of a Kind (1983), John Travolta, Olivia Newton-John.

Waiting for the Light (1990), Shirley MacLaine, Teri Garr.

Wings of Desire (1988), Bruno Ganz, Peter Falk.

APPENDIX (ii)

From puddings to pop stars, sculptures to scents...[1]

ANGEL OF THE NORTH Antony Gormley's massive metal structure of an angel with arms outstretched, which towers over the A1 on a hilltop near Newcastle.

CHARLIE'S ANGELS Seventies TV private detective glamour girls, currently being given a new lease of life in a big-screen epic.

ANGEL DELIGHT Favourite kids' dessert, comes in powder form and whips up into a frothy, sweet mousse.

ANGEL FROM BUFFY THE VAMPIRE SLAYER Handsome vampire Angel (David Boreanaz) sent to hell by Buffy but now back as a goodie with his own off-shoot series.

ANGEL PERFUME Sweet fragrance by Thierry Mugler that hit the perfume counters in 1992 and has a huge fanbase. There are 20,000 British members of his so-called Angel Circle, which you join with your first purchase.

HELL'S ANGELS Leather-clad biker clan.

HILL'S ANGELS The scantily-clad lovelies who chased Benny Hill on his Seventies TV show.

OFFICE ANGELS Secretarial employment agency.

'ANGELS' by ROBBIE WILLIAMS One of the heart-throb singer's biggest hits, recently voted the pop song most people would like played at their funeral.

APPENDIX (iii)

Suggested further reading

Anderson, Joan Wester. *Where Angels Walk* (New York: Ballantine, 1993)

Bloom, Harold. *Omens of Millennium: The Gnosis of angels, Dreams, and Resurrection*. (New York: Riverhead Books, 1996)

Bunson, Matthew. *Angels A to Z: A Who's Who of the Heavenly Host*. (New York: Crown, 1996)

Burnham, Sophy. *A Book of Angels: Reflections on Angels Past and Present and True Stories of How They Touch Our Lives*. (New York: Ballantine, 1990)

Davies, Douglas. *Death, Ritual & Belief* (Cassell; London, 1997)

Davidson, Gustav. *A Dictionary of Angels* (Free Press, 1971)

Eckersley, Glennyce. *An Angel at my Shoulder: True Stories of Angelic Experiences* (Rider Books, London 1996)

Eckersley, Glennyce. *Angels and Miracles* (Rider Books, London 1997)

Eckersley, Glennyce. *Children and Angels: True Stories of Angelic Help in times of trouble* (Rider Books, London 1999)

Eckersley, Glennyce. *Saved by the Angels* (Rider Books London 2002

Fox, Matthew and Sheldrake, Rupert. *The Physics of Angels: Exploring the Relam where Science and Spirit meet* (Harper San Francisco, 1996)

Godwin, Malcolm. *Angels: An Endangered Species*. (New York: Simon & Schuster, 1990)

Graham, Billy. *Angels: God's Secret Agents*. (New York: Doubleday, 1975)

Grubb, Nancy. *Angels in Art* (Abbeville Press, London 1995)

Burness, Carl; Burt, Alex; Hart, Justina; Mitford, John. Angels: *Millennial Messengers* (Seraphim Press, October 1999) cf. www.seraphim-press.co.uk

Lakey, Andy & Robert-Walker, Paul. *Andy Lakey: Art, Angels and Miracles* (Turner Publishing Inc.; Atlanta, 1996)

Lang, J. Stephen. *1,001 things you always wanted to know about angels, demons and the afterlife; But never thought to ask* (Thomas Nelson Publishers, October 2000)

Moody, Raymond with Perry, Paul. *Reunions: Visionary Encounters with Departed Loved Ones* (Warner Books; London, 1995)

Moolenburgh, H.C. *A Handbook of Angels* (Inland Book Co, 1989)

Price, Hope. *Angels: True Stories of how they touch our lives* (Macmillan, London, 1993)

Randles, Jennyl *The Complete Book of Aliens and Abductions* (Piatkus 1999)

Richardson, Keith. *Andy Lakey's Psychomanteum: Spiritual Journeys Guided by Art, Angels & Miracles* (Ventura Press; California, 1998)

Virtue, Doreen. *Angel Visions* (Hay House Inc, California, 2000)

ENDNOTES

Introduction

1 *Cosmopolitan Magazine* (UK Edition), December 1997, p. 36-40, 'The Extraordinary Rise and Rise of Angels'

2 'Angels Among Us', *Time Magazine*, 27 December, 1993, p. 56.

3 'Hay, David, *Religious Experience Today* (Mowbray; London, 1990), p.69

4 Website: http://www.angelhaven.com

5 For those interested, one such mail-order catalogue can be obtained from: The Angel Connection, White Stone House, 15, Grange Paddock, Mark, Nr. Highbridge, Somerset, TA9 4RW. Others also available.

6 For example, workshops run in London by Christine Astell, amongst others.

7 BBC Everyman 'Angels' – first broadcast on BBC 1, Tuesday 12 December, 2000 at 10:35 p.m.

8 Dodd, Ros, 'The trekkers who went where angels fear to tread', *The Birmingham Post*, Wednesday 25 June, 1997.

9 Niebuhr, R. Gustav, 'Long Unemployed, Angels Now Have Their Work to Do – As Guardians', *The Wall Street Journal*, 5 December, 1992, p.A1.

10 Turner, Kelly, 'Airline Pilot Photographs an Angel!', *Weekly World News*, pp. 20–1.

11 'Angels in Space', *Planetary Connection*, Issue 6, Winter 1994/5.

Chapter 2 – Touched by an angel

1 Psalm 91 v.9–12. Taken from the NRSV Bible – Catholic Edition (Thomas Nelson Publishers for Geoffrey Chapman, 1991) p. 633.

Chapter 3 – Saved!

1 Davidson, Gustav, *A Dictionary of Angels* (Free Press), p. 128.

2 Taken from an interview with myself broadcast in BBC Everyman 'Angels' – first broadcast on BBC 1, Tuesday 12 December, 2000 at 10:35 p.m

3 Gibbs, Nancy, 'Angels Among us', *Time Magazine* 27 December 1993.

4 Burnham, Sophie, *A Book of Angels* (Ballantine Books; New York, 1990), pp.49-52

5 As related to me in an interview for BBC Everyman 'Angels' – first broadcast on BBC 1, Tuesday 12 December, 2000 at 10:35 p.m.

6 For more stories of children and angel experiences, see Eckersley, Glennyce *Children and Angels* (see suggested reading list and bibliography for publisher's details).

Chapter 5 – Blind Visions

1. Adapted from Heathcote-James, Emma J. *Visionary Angelic Experiences in the Blind*, PhD. Chapter/seminar paper – 1999/2000 (unpublished paper, at time of print).

2. Ring, Kenneth PhD. ,& Cooper, Sharon M.A., 'Near-Death and Out-of-Body Experiences in the Blind: A Study of Apparent Eyeless Vision' in *Journal of Near Death Studies* 16 (2), Winter 1997 (Human Sciences Press),

3. As quoted by Stephanie in an interview with myself in BBC Everyman 'Angels' – first broadcast on BBC 1, Tuesday 12 December, 2000 at 10:35 p.m.

4. As quoted by Stephanie in an interview with myself in BBC Everyman 'Angels' – first broadcast on BBC 1, Tuesday 12 December, 2000 at 10:35 p.m.

5. Quotes have been taken from an interview between Ruth and myself on 1 October 1999.

6. *Ibid.*

7. Abridged from Ring, Kenneth Ph.D., and Cooper, Sharon M.A., 'Near-Death and Out-of-Body Experiences in the Blind: A Study of Apparent Eyeless Vision' in *Journal of Near Death Studies* 16 (2), Winter 1997 (Human Sciences Press), pp. 112–113.

8. *Ibid.*

9. Fenwick, Peter and Fenwick, Elizabeth. The Truth in the Light: An Investigation of over 300 Near Death Experiences (BCA by arrangement with Headline; London, 1995), p. 85.

10. Concar, David 'Out of Sight into Mind', New Scientist 5 September 1998, pp. 38–41.

11. Adapted from Concar, David, 'Out of Sight into Mind', New Scientist 5 September 1998, pp. 38–40.

12. Adachi, N., 'Charles Bonnet Syndrome in Leprosy; Prevalence and Clinical Characteristics' in Acta Psychiatrica Scandanavica 93(4) April 1996, Denmark, pp. 279–81.

13. Grand Rounds at Froedtert Hospital Case Presentation: Charles Bonnet Syndrome Website: http://www.grandrounds.com/NovDec97/4no6ChaBonSyn.html. Page 2 of 3.

14. *Ibid.*

15. Damas-Mora J., Skelton-Robinson M., Jenner F.A 'Charles Bonnet Syndrome in Perspective' in Psychological Medicine 12(2) May 1982, pp.2 51–61.

16 For further reading, see the Greek idea of Psychomanteums, ghosts and angels and contemporary work carried out by Prof. Douglas Davies, especially his book Death, Ritual and Belief.

17 Silverberg S, Wilansky DL., 'Scintigram in Cortial Blindness (Anton's Syndrome)' in Clinical Nuclear Medicine 3(9) September 1978, pp. 349–50.

18 Manford Mark., Andermann F., 'Complex Visual Hallucinations. Clinical and Neurobiological Insights' [Review] in Brain 121 pt.10, October 1998, pp.1819–40.

Chapter 7 – Heaven Scent

1 Medwick, Cathleen *St Teresa of Avila: The Progress of a Soul* (Alfred A. Knopf).

Chapter 8 – Angels of Mercy

1 Sylvia Gower – adapted from a version written for the *DSA (UK) Journal*, Issue 88, Summer 1998.

2 As described to me in a filmed interview on Radio West Midlands: Ed Doolan Show 19/6/00 and broadcast again in BBC Everyman 'Angels' – first broadcast on BBC 1, Tuesday 12 December, 2000 at 10:35 p.m.

Chapter 9 – Angels of Death

1 Adapted from Heathcote-James, E., Angels: Visions of Grief or Granny as your Guardian? Folklore Journal 2002 (forthcoming).

2 Davies, Douglas, Death, Ritual and Belief (Cassell; London, 1997), p. 146.

3 Ramsey, de Groot (1977).

4 Adapted from webpage http://www.after-death.com/about/adc.htm 27/3/00 Bill & Judy Guggenheim 1996-8 'What is an ADC?' p. 1.

5 Marris, P., Widows and their Families (London, RKP 1958).

6 Parkes, C.M .,Bereavement and Mental Illness (British Journal of Medical Psychology, 38, 1) (1965).

7 Rees, D, The Hallucinations of Widowhood (British Medical Journal 4), pp.37-41 and Rees, D, Death and Bereavement: The Psychological and Cultural Interfaces (Whurr; London, 1997), Chapter 17.

8 Fortean Times UnConvention, 25–26 April 1998 – University of London Union. Mark Chorvinsky is the editor of Strange Magazine.

9 http://www.apc.net/drdianne/1.htm – Website of Dianne Morrissey P.D – 9 April 2001

[10] *Ibid.*

[11] Davies, Douglas, Death, Ritual & Belief (Cassell; London, 1997), pp. 159–161.

[12] Cleiren, M., PhD, Adaptation After Bereavement (Leiden: Leiden University Press, 1991), p. 129.

[13] Finucane, R.C., Appearances of the Dead: A Cultural History of Ghosts (Junction Books: London, 1982), p. 223

[14] Morse, Melvin, 'Death-related Visions and healing Grief', taken from: http://www.death-dying.com/articles/visions.html.

Chapter 10 'Twilight Experience'

[1] Adapted from http://www.eegspectrum.com/articles/budz1977.htm Budzynski, Thomas 'Tuning in on the Twilight Zone' Reprinted from Psychology Today (August 1977).

[2] *Ibid.*

[3] Chart taken from http://www.brainsync.com/bwstates.asp 14 January 2001.

[4] Chart and boxed text taken from HYPERLINK http://www.brainsync.com/bwstates.asp http://www.brainsync.com/bwstates.asp 14 January 2001.

[5] Adapted from Guggenheim, Bill & Guggenheim, Judy, *Hello From Heaven!* (Thorsons; Harper Collins Press, London, 1996).

[6] Wells, Ron, article in The Portsdown Post, September 1997.

Tentative Conclusions

[1] Fox, Matthew, and Sheldrake, Rupert, The Physics of Angels: Exploring the Realm where Science and Physics Meet (HarperSanFrancisco, 1996).

[2] Tylor, E.B., Primitive Culture (1871: John Murrey – vol. 1.), p. 277.

[3] Heathcote, Emma, 'A Study of Narrative Angelic Experiences Through Personal Research', Undergraduate Dissertation, Department of Theology, University of Birmingham (1997) Appendix iii, figures 1–3.

[4] Ritzer, George, The McDonaldization of Society (Pine Forge Press; 1996).

[5] BARNA Research Group Ltd, Oxnard, CA, America.

[6] From: http://216.87.179.136/cgi bin/PagePressRelease.asp?PressReleaseID=3&Reference=D

[7] Taken from personal conversations with Glennyce Eckersley; same idea also reproduced by journalist Victoria Hogg, published in Cosmopolitan (December issue 1997), p. 40.

8 Including:
   http://www.yahoo.com/society_and_culture/Religion/Angels
   http://www.netangel.com/
   http://home.stlnet.com/wechsler/angel.html
   http://www.netangel.com/chat.htm
9 Appendix (ii) figure 8 – Taken from a telephone conversation with
   journalist Victoria Hogg, published in the article which I added to in
   Cosmopolitan (December issue 1997), p. 40.
10 Randles, Jenny, The Complete Book of Aliens and Abductions (Piatkus
   1999).
11 Randles, Jenny, The Complete Book of Aliens and Abductions (Piatkus
   1999), p. 125 ff.
12 Kaku, Michio, Hyperspace (Oxford Paperbacks; Reissue October, 1995).
13 Morse, Melvin, Death Related Visions and Healing Grief – a copy of
   which can be found at http://www.death-dying.com/articles/visions.html
   25 April 2001.
14 'Angels', words by R. Williams and G.Chambers.
15 Shakespeare, William, Hamlet Act I Scene V.

Results

1 Tylor, E.B., Primitive Culture (1871: John Murrey – vol. 1), p. 277.
2 Categories taken from Central Statistical Office Regional Trends 28 – A
   Publication of the Government Statistical Service (1993 Edition), ISBN:
   0261 1783, pp. 7–26.
3 Dooley, Patricia Angels (Ariel Books: Andrews and McMeel, Kansas City,
   1996), pp. 10–11.
4 Melvin Morse, available at HYPERLINK
   http://www.melvinmorse.com/light.htm
   http://www.melvinmorse.com/light.htm

Appendix (ii)

1 Adapted from: Fotheringham, Anne, *'Are angels all around us?'*, Evening
   Times (Glasgow), December 12 2000, p. 16.

Emma Heathcote-James

Bibliography
General

Adachi, N. 'Charles Bonnet Syndrome in Leprosy; Prevalence and Clinical Characteristics' in *Acta Psychiatrica Scandanavica* 93 (4) April 1996, Denmark,

Adair DK., Keshavan MS 'The Charles Bonnet Syndrome and Grief Reaction' (letter) in *American Journal of Psychiatry* 145 (7) July 1988

Anderson, Joan Wester. *Where Angels Walk.* (New York: Ballantine, 1993)

Bloom, Harold. *Omens of Millennium: The Gnosis of angels, Dreams, and Resurrection.* (New York: Riverhead Books, 1996)

Budzynski, Thomas. 'Tuning in on the Twilight Zone' from *Psychology Today* (August 1977)

Bunson, Matthew. *Angels A to Z: A Who's Who of the Heavenly Host.* (New York: Crown, 1996)

Burness, Carl; Burt, Alex; Hart, Justina; Mitford, John. *Angels: Millennial Messengers* (Seraphim Press, October 1999) cf. www.seraphim-press.co.uk

Burnham, Sophy. *A Book of Angels: Reflections on Angels Past and Present and True Stories of How They Touch Our Lives.* (New York: Ballantine, 1990)

Cleiren, M. PhD. *Adaptation After Bereavement* (Leiden: Leiden University Press, 1991)

Concar, David. 'Out of Sight into Mind' in *New Scientist* 5 September 1998 (ICI Press) pp. 38–41

Cogan, D.G. 'Visual Hallucinations as release phenomena' in *Albrecht Von Graefes Achiv fur Klinische und Experimentelle Ophthalmologie* 188 (2) 23 August 1973

Damas-Mora J.; Skelton-Robinson M.; Jenner F.A. 'Charles Bonnet Syndrome in Perspective' in *Psychological Medicine* 12 (2) May 1982

Daniel, Alma; Wyllie, Timothy and Ramer, Andrew. *Ask Your Angels.* (New York: Ballantine, 1992)

Davidson, Gustav. *A Dictionary of Angels* (Free Press, 1971)

Davies, Douglas. *Death, Ritual & Belief* (Cassell; London, 1997)

Doyle, Sir Arthur Conan. *History of Spiritualism* (1926)

Doyle, Sir Arthur Conan (ed.). Life and Mission of Home – Scotland and America D.D Home, His life and Mission: Mme Dunglas Home *(Trench, Trunber and Co. Ltd., London 1921)*

Eckersley, Glennyce S. *An Angel at my Shoulder: True Stories of Angelic Experiences* (Rider Books, London 1996)

Eckersley, Glennyce S. *Angels and Miracles* (Rider Books, London 1997)

Eckersley, Glennyce S. *Children and Angels: True Stories of Angelic Help in times of trouble* (Rider Books, London 1999)

Seeing Angels

Fearheiley, Don. *Angels Among Us* (Avon Books, 1993)

Fenwick, Peter and Fenwick, Elizabeth. *The Truth in the Light: An Investigation of over 300 Near Death Experiences* (BCA by arrangement with Headline; London, 1995)

Finucane, R.C. *Appearances of the Dead: A Cultural History of Ghosts* (Junction Books: London, 1982)

Gross, Richard D. *Psychology: The Science of Mind and Behaviour - 2nd Edition* (Hodder and Stoughton; London 1993 – 5th imprint

Garret, Duane A. *Angels and the New Spirituality.* (Nashville: Broadman and Holman, 1995)

Gittelston, Bernard. *PSI and Mind Intangible Evidence* (Fireside, Simon & Schuster, New York, 1987)

Godwin, Malcolm. *Angels: An Endangered Species.* (New York: Simon & Schuster, 1990)

Gonzales-Wippler, Migene. *Santeria, the Religion: A Legacy of Faith, Rites, and Magic.* (New York: Harmony Books, 1989)

Graham, Billy. *Angels: God's Secret Agents.* (New York: Doubleday, 1975)

Grey, Cameron, ed. *Angels and Awakenings: Stories of the Miraculous by Great Modern Writers.* (Rockland, MA: Wheeler Publishing, 1980)

Grubb, Nancy. *Angels in Art* (Abbeville Press, London 1995)

Guiley, Rosemary Ellen. *Angels Of Mercy.* (Out of print)

Guggenheim, Bill & Guggenheim, Judy. *Hello From Heaven!* (Harper Collins Press; London, 1996)

Kaku, Michio. *Hyperspace* (Oxford Paperbacks; reissue October, 1995)

Kent, Jack A. *The Psychological Origins of the resurrection Myth* (Open Gate Press: London, 1999)

Kipp, Eva. *The Water Angel's Love: A Nepalese Tale* (Book Faith India; Delhi, 1999)

Lakey, Andy & Robert-Walker, Paul. *Andy Lakey: Art, Angels and Miracles* (Turner Publishing Inc.; Atlanta, 1996)

Lampl, A.W and Oliver, G.W. (Los Angeles). *'Vision without Sight'* in *Journal of Analytical Psychology* (Number 30, 1995)

Lawson, David. *A Company of Angels: Your Angel transformation Guide* (Findhorn Press; Scotland 1998)

Lewis, James R. and Evelyn Dorothy Oliver. *Angels A to Z.* (Detroit: Visible Ink Press, 1996)

McNamara, M.E.; Heros, R.C.; Boller, F. *'Visual Hallucinations in Blindness: The Charles Bonnet Syndrome'* in *International Journal of Neuroscience* 17(1) July 1982

Malz, Betty. *Angels Watching over me* (Revell Fleming H Co, 1986)

Manford Mark., Andermann F., 'Complex Visual Hallucinations. Clinical and Neurobiological Insights' [Review] in *Brain* 121 pt.10, *October 1998*

MaeGregor, Geddes. *Angels: Ministers of Grace.* (New York: Paragon, 1988)

Margolies, Morris B. *A Gathering of Angels: Angels in Jewish Life and Literature.* (New York: Ballantine, 1994)

Mark, Barbara, with Trudy Griswold. *Angelspeake.* (New York: Simon and Schuster, 1995)

Marris, P. *Widows and their Families* (London, RKP 1958)

Martin-Kuri, K. *A Message For The Millennium.* (New York: Ballantine Books, 1996)

Melton, J. Gordon. *Encyclopaedic Handbook of Cults in America.* (New York: Garland Publishing, 1986)

Medwick, Cathleen. *St Teresa of Avila: The Progress of a Soul* (Alfred A. Knopf)

Moody, Raymond with Perry, Paul. *Reunions: Visionary Encounters with Departed Loved Ones* (Warner Books; London, 1995)

Moolenburgh, H.C. *A Handbook of Angels* (Inland Book Co, 1989)

Morris B. *A Gathering of Angels: Angels in Jewish Life and Literature* (Ballantine Trade, 1994)

Muhammed. Shaykh and Kabbani, Hisham. *Angels Unveiled: A Sufi Perspective* (Kazi Publications, Chicago 1995)

Pagels, Elaine. *The Origin of Satan.* (New York: Random House, 1995)

Parkes, C.M. 'Bereavement and Mental Illness' in *British Journal of Medical Psychology*, 38, (1) 1965

Parkes, C.M. & Weiss, R.S. *Recovery from Bereavement* (Basic Books; New York, 1983)

Peatfield RC., Rose FC., 'Migrainous visual symptoms in a woman without eyes' in *Archives of Neurology* 38(7) July 1981

Price, Hope. *Angels: True Stories of how they touch our lives* (Macmillan, London, 1993)

Price, Jonathan Randolph. *Angels Within Us.* (Faweett Books, 1993)

Randles, Jenny. *The Complete Book of Aliens and Abductions* (Piatkus 1999)

Richardson, Keith. *Andy Lakey's Psychomanteum: Spiritual Journeys Guided by Art, Angels & Miracles* (Ventura Press; California, 1998)

Ring, Kenneth Ph.D. and Cooper, Sharon M.A. 'Near-Death and Out-of-Body Experiences in the Blind: A Study of Apparent Eyeless Vision' in *Journal of Near Death Studies* 16 (2), Winter 1997 (Human Sciences Press)

Ritzer, George. *The McDonaldization of Society* (Pine Forge Press; 1996)

Ronan, Margaret. *Strange, Unsolved Mysteries.* (Scholastic Book Service, 1974)

Schultz G.; Needham W.; Taylor R.; Shindell S.; Melzack R. 'Properties of

Seeing Angels

Complex Hallucinations Associated with Deficits in Vision' in *Perception* 25(6) 1996

Fox, Matthew and Sheldrake, Rupert. *The Physics of Angels: Exploring the Realm where science and physics meet* (HarperSanFrancisco, 1996)

Silverberg S.; Wilansky, D.L. 'Scintigram in Cortial Blindness (Anton's Syndrome)' in *Clinical Nuclear Medicine* 3(9) September 1978, pp. 349–50

Taylor, R.E.; Mancil, G.L.; Kramer, S.H. 'Visual Hallucinations: Meaning and Management' in *Journal of the American Optomeric Association* 57(12) December 1986, pp. 889–892

Taylor, Terry Lynn, with Mary Beth Crain. *Angel Wisdom.* (HarperSan Francisco, 1994)

Virtue, Doreen. *Angel Visions* (Hay House Inc, California, 2000)

Virtue, Doreen. *Divine Guidance: How to have Conversations With God and Your Guardian*

Webber, William D. Marily. *A Rustle of Angels : Stories About Angels in Real Life and Scripture* (Zondervan Pub House, 1994)

White, C.P.; Jan J.E. 'Visual Hallucinations after acute visual loss in a young child' in *Developmental Medicine and Child Neurology* 34(3) March 1992, pp. 259–261.

White, N.J. 'Complex Visual Hallucinations in Partial Blindness Due to Eye Disease' in *British Journal of Psychiatry* 136 March 1980, pp. 284–286

White, Ruth. *Working with Guides and Angels* (Piatkus Ltd, London 1996)

Acknowledgements

Who would have thought almost five years ago, when I originally began a simple project on angelic experiences in Great Britain, that it would have expanded in to doctoral research? As a result, the data and findings have filled countless newspaper and magazine pages, radio programmes, a documentary and at last this book. I now feel it is time to close the cover on this research. It has been a fabulous journey from beginning to end in which I have had the most amazing opportunities and met some truly wonderful people.

Dr. Martin Stringer, my long-suffering supervisor, must be thanked first and foremost – without him, this idea would never have got off the ground. Thanks, Martin, for putting up with my passion and enthusiasm for the topic and for all your humour, friendship and boundless back-up throughout every adventure undertaken! Of course, those thanks extends to all colleagues and students within the Theology Department at The University of Birmingham.

Big thanks to 'Hector' for your companionship throughout and the long walks! To Leon, my parents, Dick, Dave, Jus, Harriet and Tiegs and of course to Gran and Gramps Giles, to whom this book is dedicated – thank you all for putting up with me and the accompanied angelmania that has somewhat crept into and surrounded our lives these past few years!

To all my friends, especially Alice Bullock, Claire Brown, Nick Plowright, Naomi Trenear, Alix West, Kim and Maurice, Kate Philpot, John-Francis, Glennyce Eckersley, Steve Hopley and Keith Bishop. To Gay Pilgrim, who read through the first draft of this, and for all her wise words, help and support along the way. Without all you guys, and the others I've failed to mention – your friendship and laughter has been, and is, so appreciated. To Norman Hull and Maggie for seeing the potential in this study and to everyone who was involved cover to cover in creating the Everyman documentary, and for introducing me to another world outside academia.

Thanks goes to all at Blake Publishing – to Rosie and John, Adam, Michelle, James; to Rob Dimery, and everyone else who has been a part of making this book. To John Mitford and Alex Birt for the cover and the fabulous piccies and of course to Krispy for having introduced us in the first place!

To everyone who has expressed interest in this work, broadcast and print journalists, as well as the various groups, societies, schools and universities where I have presented the findings – with special mention to Steve Morris and the Theology Society at Bedford Boys' School. I could go on forever – in all, so many people have supported me and have been there along the way that there are too many to mention individually by name.

Finally, my greatest thanks, appreciation and acknowledgement goes to everyone who has taken the time over the past few years to write to me and share their individual experiences. My only regret is having not met all of you in person to be able to thank you. Those who have kept in correspondence I thank for their interest and support. Because of time and space, this book only contains the first 350 accounts received, and I thank all those, especially for their willingness and permission for me to share them with you. To them and the other 500 or so whose letters I have here filed beside me: without you, neither my university work, nor indeed this very book you are holding, would exist…